The Teacher's Introduction to

ATTACHMENT

of related interest

Observing Children with Attachment Difficulties in School
A Tool for Identifying and Supporting Emotional and
Social Difficulties in Children Aged 5–11
*Kim S. Golding, Jane Fain, Ann Frost, Cathy Mills, Helen Worrall,
Netty Roberts, Eleanor Durrant and Sian Templeton*
ISBN 978 1 84905 336 5
eISBN 978 0 85700 675 2

Observing Children with Attachment Difficulties in Preschool Settings
A Tool for Identifying and Supporting Emotional and Social Difficulties
Kim S. Golding, Jane Fain, Ann Frost, Sian Templeton and Eleanor Durrant
Foreword by Louise Bombèr
ISBN 978 1 84905 337 2
eISBN 978 085700 676 9

Attachment, Trauma, and Healing
Understanding and Treating Attachment Disorder
in Children and Families
Second Edition
Terry M. Levy and Michael Orlans
ISBN 978 1 84905 888 9
eISBN 978 0 85700 597 7

**A Short Introduction to Attachment
and Attachment Disorder**
Colby Pearce
ISBN 978 1 84310 957 0
eISBN 978 1 84642 949 1

Attachment in Common Sense and Doodles
A Practical Guide
Miriam Silver
Foreword by Camila Batmanghelidjh
ISBN 978 1 84905 314 3
eISBN 978 0 85700 624 0

Can I tell you about Adoption?
A guide for friends, family and professionals
Anne Braff Brodzinsky
ISBN 978 1 84905 942 8
eISBN 978 0 85700 759 9

Adopted Like Me
My Book of Adopted Heroes
Ann Angel
ISBN 978 1 84905 935 0
ISBN 978 0 85700 740 7

The Teacher's Introduction to
ATTACHMENT

Practical Essentials for Teachers, Carers and School Support Staff

Nicola Marshall

Foreword Phil Thomas

Jessica Kingsley *Publishers*
London and Philadelphia

First published in 2014
by Jessica Kingsley Publishers
73 Collier Street
London N1 9BE, UK
and
400 Market Street, Suite 400
Philadelphia, PA 19106, USA

www.jkp.com

Library of Congress Cataloging in Publication Data
Marshall, Nicola.
  The teacher's introduction to attachment : practical essentials for teachers, carers and
school support
staff / Nicola Marshall, Phil Thomas.
      pages cm
  Includes bibliographical references and index.
  ISBN 978-1-84905-550-5 (alk. paper)
  1. Problem children--Education. 2. Psychic trauma in children. 3. Attachment
disorder in children. I.
Title.
  LC4801.M364 2014
  371.93--dc23
                                    2014010522

British Library Cataloguing in Publication Data
A CIP catalogue record for this book is available from the British Library

ISBN 978 1 84905 550 5
eISBN 978 0 85700 973 9

Printed and bound in Great Britain

CONTENTS

FOREWORD

In my experience as a teacher-come-head teacher, I have come across many so-called hard-to-reach children. Teachers, with their multiplicity of skills and strategies, will use every established tool within their grasp – and many that they just seem to pull out of nowhere – to manage children presenting challenging or non-compliant behaviour. But there comes a time when you've tried all the tricks in the book and you feel you have failed. Not just yourself – you feel you have failed the child.

Dysfunctional or disaffected behaviour is often more than just that. A child who is proving hard to reach is often trying to either protect himself, or crying out for help, or both. All too often, we can miss this and the opportunity to help the child is lost and their hurt is deepened through our lack of understanding.

I wish I had read Nicola's book when I first trained as a teacher. The children we, as teachers, remember the most are more often than not the most challenging ones. Wouldn't it be great if we could look back and say that we had made a positive difference to every single one of those children? However, I am ashamed to say that, for me at least, that has not always been the case.

Nicola's book addresses, in particular, the challenge of children who have experienced early trauma – either through domestic violence and a string of foster parents or other experiences, which hinder the essential nurturing of those early years. She systematically unwraps the layers that help to reveal and make sense of the hurt – and behaviour patterns – of children who have experienced early trauma. She then carefully guides us through proven and evidence-based strategies to get through to the hard-to-reach child and begin to rebuild and repair the broken pieces of his life.

I found this book enormously helpful and also reassuring. It bolstered up my toolkit of resources to understand and help the vulnerable children I come across – and it reassured me that I am equipped to help: those children I think are hard to reach are actually within my reach and I could be the person to help them.

I thoroughly recommend Nicola's book: as an adoptive parent, Nicola has a wealth of experience – and many a story to tell – and she shares it all in a compassionate and intelligent style, making it an accessible book for all.

Phil Thomas
Teacher, Head Teacher and Resilience Trainer (ThinQ Education)

ACKNOWLEDGEMENTS

On my journey to write this book there have been many individuals who have contributed to its completion; I would like to mention a few.

First, to my colleague, friend and editor Phil Thomas, as an Educational Professional himself. It was important for me to have someone who could review this book from a very practical point of view, so that those reading will get the most from these pages. Thank you Phil for your tireless editing and continual encouragement of my work in this field, as well as your brilliant Foreword.

My family (especially my three adopted children) are not only encouraging and supportive in my writing endeavours, but are of course my muses. Their relentless bravery inspires me and I long to see how they will navigate through the next challenging season in their lives.

My final acknowledgement is to the many teachers, teaching assistants, head teachers, SENCOs and learning mentors who have attended my courses over the last three years. Without their dedication to learning more about these children, there would be hundreds of children struggling to engage with our narrow educational system. My dream is that someday our system will provide enough flexibility for *all* students to learn, in whatever way they need to, to be able to function in life and become well-rounded and giving adults.

INTRODUCTION

Let me introduce you to Fruit Bat 1, 2 and 3. These are the affectionate nicknames we have for our three adorable, adopted children. They are the reason for this book. Since they have come into our lives, they have opened our eyes to the world of attachment and trauma. Their resilience along with their vulnerability has touched my heart and given me a mission to try to help others understand the impact of trauma on children.

As you have chosen to read this book, I assume you too have an interest in this area. Whether you work with children who have experienced trauma in their lives, you live with a vulnerable child or you are a professional who tries to help these children in some other way, the fact that you have opened this book tells me you are keen to know more.

> *The key to most things in life is awareness and understanding. Once you have that, the strategies are easier to find.*

This book will be a down-to-earth, practical and accessible look at this world of attachment and trauma, particularly in educational settings. There will, of course, be some theory so that you can understand the fundamental emotional and physical impact of trauma on a child. However, I hope you will find it comes from a real place of experience – heart knowledge, not just head knowledge.

This book is divided into four parts. Part 1 is focused more on the theories around attachment, drawing from some of the experts in the field of attachment. My hope is that, as you read, you will be inspired to learn more and, to that end, you will find a resource list in the back of this book.

Part 2 concentrates on some guiding principles to follow when working with these children. There will be strategies in this part but also very loose principles and guidelines so that you can adapt this to your own setting. You already have a vast experience and knowledge of children that you can call on and, once you can see the world through the eyes of these children, who are topsy-turvy in their thinking and approach to the world, then I believe you will be able to connect to them in a more real and relevant way.

Part 3 of this book takes a closer look at certain common issues for children who have experienced trauma. This part is a reference for you as the children you work with present behaviours that surprise and astound you. They may be subtle sometimes, overt at other times, but every behaviour you see is communicating a need to you.

Once you can speak the language of attachment you will see the fear and pain these children live with, day in and day out.

As they feel safe with you, they may reveal more of the anxiety and difficulties they have.

Part 4 is just some final thoughts – some things to be aware of and to mull over in your interactions with these children. In all honesty they are things I wanted to include but they didn't fit in the other three parts!

Since I have started studying this world of attachment and trauma, and living the daily impacts, I have come to realise it is a never-ending quest for knowledge, understanding and exploring new strategies. My aim is that, as you read this book, it will spark ideas and areas of interest for you as you travel this minefield of a journey. You can read this book from beginning to end, or you can dip in and out of the resources and reference guide as the children you work with bring more complex issues to you.

Above all, I would like to say thank you *to you for your commitment and dedication to these children.*

As a parent, I am forever grateful to those who want to really engage and connect with my children in a way that will impact them forever. Whether you really know the impact you have on these children or not – *you do have an impact.* Every moment they spend away from their home environment and with other adults is an opportunity to develop the skills they need to be able to function as strong, capable adults. The more people who can help break the cycle they have come from, the better. All of us, as a society, need to understand the responsibility we have to teach our children how to be resilient and to engage with the world around them. As much as we want them to learn the academics of life, if they do not learn how to connect, to have empathy and to be resilient, they will not learn how to contribute to their communities, to hold down jobs, to maintain strong, sound relationships and to be good enough parents themselves in the future.

So enjoy this book and I hope it takes you on an incredible journey of discovery as you endeavour to understand the world of attachment and trauma. It's a long journey, and this is just the beginning, but it's well worth the ride!

Part I

THE THEORY BEHIND ATTACHMENT AND TRAUMA

Chapter 1

WHAT IS TRAUMA?

Some of children's behaviour in the classroom can be very strange and confusing: the child who seems to crave negative attention, the explosive outbursts of seemingly otherwise placid children, the hiding under tables or biting sleeves of clothes. How about the child who goes through their whole primary school experience without ever being invited to another child's birthday party? Or a child fixated on a particular teaching assistant – so much so that they cry when they have to leave them? What about the otherwise intelligent child who cannot grasp the implications of spitting at other children, or the child in reception who has to be home-schooled because of her very challenging behaviour?

How about the high school girl who lines up the yellow cards in front of her – proud of her achievement of being told off more than anyone else in the classroom? Have you noticed that very sensitive ten-year-old boy who cries whenever he loses his pencil or someone looks at him in a funny way? How about the 15-year-old who seems to always be the one caught stealing – even though his 'friends' put him up to it? Do you notice the small 11-year-old girl in Year 7 who doesn't seem to be able to connect with the others around her and gravitates towards the other vulnerable children?

These are all real examples of children I know – children who struggle in our educational system. They don't trust people; they don't make deep lasting relationships. Learning is not why they come to school; they come because we make them. Whilst they are there their main aim is to survive the day – to come out unscathed to live another day. This may sound very dramatic but I know it is true of many vulnerable children.

What are these behaviours about? What are these children trying to say to us through their actions? We need to take a big step back and look at what may have happened in their lives before they came to school to really understand what the feelings are behind the behaviour they present to us.

In order to take this step back you need to first understand the impact of trauma.

There are two elements that need to be present for trauma to occur. The first is an external event, incident or threat to a person. This may be in the form of an actual attack on a person, through domestic violence, for example, where a child is physically hit. It may also be through the atmosphere of a threatening environment where an adult is hit, shouted at or emotionally abused – where a child is surrounded by that ever-present feeling of dread.

The other element is the internal response to that threat. Depending on many factors such as our personalities, resilience and perceptions of a situation, the internal response will be different and can span the full range of emotions. This is why you may have two siblings in a family that experience the same threatening environment but respond very differently.

> Trauma is, by definition, a combination of an external event and an internal experience. (Cairns 2002)

There are also two types of trauma. The first type (type I) is where the external event is a one off: it may be a violent attack, bereavement, having witnessed something horrible or having a major accident. The second (type II) is repetitive trauma, where the external event or threat is on an on-going basis – this is what we are talking about primarily in this book. It is important to note, though, that children who experience type I trauma may still experience the long-term effects of trauma described in later chapters of this book. The internal response is the key. The episode may have been so devastating to the child that the impact is long-lasting.

When thinking about trauma, it is important to consider what these external factors actually look like and where they can come from. The factors surrounding the trauma and how that impacts a child can be complex, and Chapter 2 will outline some of those areas of risk.

Chapter 2

WHAT CAUSES TRAUMA?

ABUSE AND NEGLECT

Probably the most talked about area, abuse and neglect are sadly things we hear too much about these days. Abuse falls into many categories such as physical abuse (domestic violence), sexual abuse, emotional and mental abuse. Again, when we think about the direct threat and the perceived threat, this can be actual abuse against the child or against others within the environment that the child witnesses on a daily basis.

Take domestic violence, for example. Consider for a moment someone you love being hurt in a room next door: you can hear them being hurt, you can feel the fear and devastation but you cannot do anything to prevent their pain. That helplessness and powerlessness is something children living with domestic violence experience continually – the sense of fear and shame of not being able to stop the abuse.

Neglect is something that came very much to the forefront of our minds many years ago when the orphanages in Romania and Russia were discovered. Horrendous images of row upon row of children in cots with no stimulation, no physical contact and no nurture brought a sick feeling to all our stomachs. In this day and age, we would be horrified to think that still exists. However, it does!

The statistics on neglect in children in the UK published by the NSPCC (National Society for the Prevention of Cruelty to Children) tell us:

- 21,312 children were the subject of a child protection plan under the category of neglect or were on a child protection register under a category that includes neglect on 31 March 2013.

- 42 per cent of all the children in the UK who were the subject of a child protection plan or on a child protection register were under a category that includes neglect.

Another area of abuse occurs when the pregnant mother has been drinking alcohol or taking drugs during pregnancy.

This is a whole area in itself and one worth exploring more: Foetal Alcohol Spectrum Disorder is very similar to attachment difficulties in its symptoms but requires a different approach.

In the resource section of this book, you will find places to research this more. The statistics again are frightening in this area:

> When you drink, so does your baby. It takes approximately one hour for your body to process each unit of alcohol; it takes 3 times as long for the alcohol to pass round the system of the baby in the womb. (FASD Trust website)

There is much debate about how much is too much in terms of drinking alcohol during pregnancy. The impact on the unborn child depends very much on the amount of alcohol and the time period during the pregnancy. However, below you will find a list of the potential problems newborns could face as a result of alcohol misuse during pregnancy, according to the Missouri Department of Mental Health, Division of Alcohol and Drug Abuse:

- small body size and weight

- slower than normal development and failure to 'catch up'

- deformed ribs and sternum

- curved spine and hip dislocations

- bent, fused, webbed, or missing fingers or toes

- limited movement of joints

- small head

- facial abnormalities

- small eye openings

- skin webbing between eyes and base of nose

- drooping eyelids
- near-sightedness
- failure of eyes to move in same direction
- short upturned nose
- sunken nasal bridge
- flat or absent groove between nose and upper lip
- thin upper lip
- opening in roof of mouth
- small jaw
- low-set or poorly formed ears
- organ deformities
- heart defects or heart murmurs
- genital malformations
- kidney and urinary defects
- central nervous system handicaps
- small brain
- faulty arrangement of brain cells and connective tissue
- mental retardation – occasionally severe
- learning disabilities
- short attention span
- irritability in infancy
- hyperactivity in childhood
- poor body, hand and finger coordination.

A sobering list!

SEPARATION FROM BIRTH MOTHER

In her book, *The Primal Wound*, Nancy Verrier (2009) talks about the inexplicable bond we have with our mother. That primal connection with the person who gave us life is a very misunderstood phenomenon.

> *Many times I have heard people say that if a baby is taken away from its mother at birth there will be no impact on the child in the future – this is not the case.*

The separation from the person who gave us life is itself a trauma. If you speak to adoptees who may have been born in the 1960s when voluntary relinquishments were commonplace, you will hear the struggles they had throughout their lives with the feeling of not knowing who they were and where they came from.

In her book, Nancy Verrier quotes a story from *Necessary Losses* by Judith Viorst (1986 p.10):

> A young boy lies in a hospital bed. He is frightened and in pain. Burns cover 40% of his small body. Someone has doused him with alcohol and then, unimaginably, has set him on fire.
>
> He cries for his mother.
>
> His mother has set him on fire.
>
> It doesn't seem to matter what kind of mother a child has lost, or how perilous it may be to dwell in her presence. It doesn't matter whether she hurts or hugs. Separation from mother is worse than being in her arms when the bombs are exploding. Separation from mother is sometimes worse than being with her when she is the bomb.

Nancy Verrier goes on to say:

> I am not suggesting that we keep a child with a mother who will set him on fire, but I am suggesting that we have to understand what we are doing when we take him away from her.

MULTIPLE HOME AND SCHOOL MOVES

Another area that impacts a child's attachment and development is around the number of moves they endure in their lives. If a child is adopted in the UK, they will have experienced at least two very traumatic moves: one from their birth family and then again from their foster carers. That is the best-case scenario – many times children are moved around different foster carers time and time again. I have heard of children as young as ten months old having ten moves, one a month, in their very short lives. Our eldest child had five moves of nursery and school before the age of seven – the impact of that is huge on her learning and development.

For a moment, imagine your current lifestyle: your job, house, partner or family and friends, car – everything that makes up your daily existence. Now imagine I plucked you from that life and placed you somewhere else – a new car, a bigger house, a more loving partner, family, friends, a better paid job. The only proviso is that you cannot have anything to do with your current life again – no contact and no chance to return. That is what happens many times for these children. It is the right thing to do to move them from a dangerous environment, but *we should never underestimate the impact these moves have on children.* Of course they will feel unsettled, scared and distrustful of adults as they are continually let down and moved on.

BORN PREMATURE OR POSTNATAL DEPRESSION

Whilst these are not easy areas to consider, as often they are nobody's fault, we still have to acknowledge them as a risk factor. Consider a baby born premature and the environment they are born into when compared to a baby born full term: the incubator, the lack of touch and eye contact, the sterile environment and the trauma that the baby may have gone through during labour – these can all contribute to a stressed baby.

In many cases, when you consider postnatal depression, there is another adult who supports the mum and baby: a partner, a friend, their own mother. However, the danger occurs when there is not that support structure – a single mum for example or a mum in a domestic violence environment where there is no support. The baby then lacks the stimulus needed in those very crucial early months of life. This can have a lasting impact on a baby.

When considering the factors that may create trauma for a child, it's worth noting that this can occur as early as being in the womb. Many times, we think about these things happening to a child when they are a toddler but there are events that greatly affect a child that may have happened before they were even born – pre-birth stress for the mother, for example. When we experience stress, our bodies release a chemical called cortisol. In a mother, this chemical flows through her system and transfers to the baby. If you think about a stressed pregnant woman in an environment of domestic violence, the cortisol they release would be intense. This transferred to a baby in the womb means that, when born, the resting heart rate and stress level for that child will be different to a child who has not experienced that level of stress.

It's worth stating again here though that we have to remember the two factors needed to create trauma: the external experience and the internal response. Whatever the risk factors may be for a child at any age, each child is different – the way they perceive the experiences they have are very different. You could have ten children from the same family and see ten different responses to that environment. All are important and all relevant and crucial to be aware of and to try to understand.

POVERTY

This may not be something that's normally included in a list like this but I feel it is important to mention. One of the books I highly recommend is *The Kid* by Kevin Lewis (2003). It's his autobiography and it tells the incredibly sad but inspiring story of his life. Born to a family living in poverty and filth, Kevin experienced terrible hunger, deprivation and horrendous living conditions – not to mention the domestic violence in the home. It is a harrowing story and one you can't believe takes place today, but it does. Kevin was born in 1970 – the same year as me – and I can't imagine what his life was like during those early years.

One of the aspects of the book really stuck with me is the long-lasting effect the deprivation has on Kevin. Even much later in life, when he makes a new life for himself, he talks about the impact of not having enough food in his early years and the continual problems he experienced with food as a result.

Most of the adopted children I know have issues around food. I'm not saying they all came from this level of poverty but they definitely have issues about there being enough food, what kind of food, if someone will take their food, and so on.

Some 18 per cent of children in the UK – that's over two million – live below the poverty line, say the official figures. However, professionals within the field see things differently:

> The reality is that there are 3.6 million children growing up in poverty in the UK, children without a winter coat or going to bed hungry, and this number is set to grow. (Justin Forsyth, Chief Executive, Save the Children 2012)

The added problem for those in poverty is of course that these pressures can lead to other risks that can create trauma for a child, such as in the case of Kevin Lewis: alcohol abuse, aggression and violence within the home.

LONG-TERM ILLNESS OR HOSPITALISATION

Again this is probably not something you might expect to be in a list like this but I have known cases of children who have experienced prolonged illness, had to have operations or spent long stays in hospital away from their parents. These children invariably wrestle with the impact that a long-term condition can have on them emotionally as well as physically. There is of course the added confusion when a child is in physical pain and the parents are there with them – how confusing must that be to have your protector with you and it seems they are not protecting you?

The symptoms you will see later on in this book around attachment can also be seen in children who have experienced long-term conditions.

Chapter 3

WHAT IS ATTACHMENT?

So what is this thing we call Attachment Theory? The impact of insecure attachment is also sometimes referred to as developmental trauma, reactive attachment disorder (RAD), disinhibited attachment disorder (DAD), childhood trauma disorder, social and emotional difficulties – the list goes on.

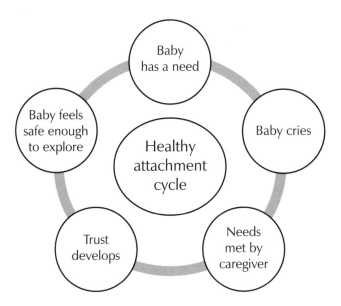

Figure 3.1 Healthy attachment cycle.

Figure 3.1 shows the attachment cycle in a healthy baby. You can see that when a baby has a need, he makes that need known to his caregiver and, more often than not, that need is met. What then happens for the baby is trust starts to develop. The baby knows that he is OK, that the world is OK and that his needs will be met. The baby can then calm down, feel regulated and the cycle continues. He also starts to realise he is safe and can explore the world around him.

However, in a disturbed attachment cycle (Figure 3.2), the baby's needs are invariably not met or are very inconsistently and inappropriately met; for example, if a baby is hungry, he may sometimes be fed, but, at other times, the baby may be ignored or shouted at. The baby then starts to feel rage instead of trust; he begins to feel unsafe and he believes that the world is not a safe place to be. The effects of that are that the baby starts to internalise that feeling as shame, that he is bad and the world around him is bad. He cannot self-regulate as a result. That is why you may hear a parent say that the baby doesn't cry very much any more; this may be because the child has already made the decision subconsciously that his needs will not be met, so he gives up.

It is normal for a baby to cry: we are born as needy human beings, with the instinct to rely on others – to be dependent on others to meet our needs.

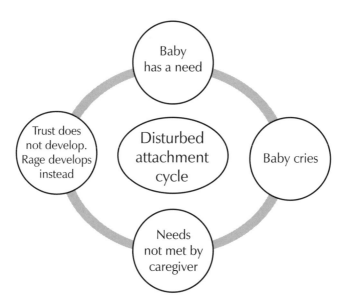

Figure 3.2 Disturbed attachment cycle.

This cycle may seem like a very simplistic model but most of what happens between a baby and its primary caregiver are tiny moments of connection: a look, a smile and touch – things that we take for granted. However, if you have been around a mother who is struggling to connect with her baby, or has so much stress in her own life that she cannot focus on the child, you will probably have seen the impact on the child.

This impact will be explored in much more detail throughout this book, but, for now, notice newborns around you and how they come alive when an adult connects with them, and you can see the way a baby copies the adult and forms a strong bond with them.

Chapter 4

ATTACHMENT THEORISTS

Attachment Theory has developed over a number of years. John Bowlby is known as the father of attachment. Born in London in 1907, he was the fourth of six siblings. His parents were considered upper-middle-class and, as was the custom in those days, John was raised primarily by nannies and, as such, had little contact with his parents. He was later sent to boarding school at the age of seven. Bowlby did have one particular nanny he was quite attached to up until the age of four and then she left the family, which left an emotional scar on Bowlby – he describes this as similar to the loss of a mother.

As a result of his own early experiences, John Bowlby started his research into the effects of early separation and loss on life-long development. Through his research, his first two conclusions were:

1. separation from primary caregivers leads to life-long struggles for individuals and

2. the emotional attitudes of parents towards the children have life-shaping effects.

When a baby is born he cannot tell one person from another and indeed can hardly tell person from thing. Yet, by his first birthday he is likely to have become a connoisseur of people. Not only does he come quickly to distinguish familiars he chooses one or more favourites. They are greeted with delight; they are followed when they depart; and they are sought when absent. Their loss causes anxiety and distress; their recovery, relief and a sense of security. On this foundation, it seems, the rest of his emotional life is built – without this foundation there is risk for his future happiness and health. (Bowlby 1967, p.17)

John Bowlby came against opposition within the industry, as he had no scientific proof of his theories about mental health and emotional wellbeing. All he had were his life-long observations of families and children.

At about the same time, another research study was taking place, which started to add some scientific weight to Bowlby's studies: Harlow's rhesus monkeys. This first scientific experiment in 1958 demonstrated, in many cases, the monkey's need for warmth and comfort over food. This indicated that our basic needs as humans are more than just food and water; there is also a driving need for interaction, affection and the comfort of another.

Throughout the 1950s and 1960s, Bowlby's work attracted more interest. In the late 1950s, he had his work published in some prominent papers and his theories still remain the foundation of modern Attachment Theory today.

Next came Mary Ainsworth, who was a student of Bowlby's. Unlike Bowlby, Mary Ainsworth had a happy childhood. However, she still felt insecurities, which led her to pursue a career questioning secure attachments and childhood. She is best known for her observation of infants and parents in their home environment, which again was contrary to common practice at the time. After some years of intensive study and research with mothers and babies, she developed a study she named the Strange Situation Study. It was a 20-minute observation involving parent and child in an unfamiliar room. They then go through a series of changes involving parent leaving, stranger entering and parent re-entering. All the time the child is observed on two levels:

1. the amount of exploration the child engages in throughout the study and

2. the child's reactions to the departure and re-entry of the parent.

Mary herself says of her work:

> I did not intend this as a way of assessing attachment, but it certainly wound up as that. We began to realise that it fit in with our impressions after seventy-two hours of observation in an amazing way. But instead of seventy-two hours of observation we could do a Strange Situation in twenty minutes. (Mary Ainsworth, from Karen 1998 in Garhart Mooney *Theories of Attachment*, 2010, p.25)

Another study of note was by Dr Edward Tronick, a renowned researcher and teacher on neuro-behavioural and social emotional development of infants and young children, who, in 1975, ran an experiment known as the Still Face Experiment. This was done with a mother and baby. The mother and baby interact in a normal way: eye contact, lots of sounds and smiles, cooing and touches. The baby responds to the mother's stimulation and smiles and laughs back at her. Halfway through this interaction, the mother changes her approach and adopts a blank expression – no eye contact and no interaction with the baby. The baby is visibly distressed by this change. She tries to engage her mum in any way she can – smiling, laughing, pointing and then, as she gets more confused and distressed, she starts to arch her back and scream.

Once the mother re-engages with the baby the child calms down straight away and all is well again. This was a powerful reflection of the effects of those nurturing actions that all babies need to develop and feel safe in the world. The fact that a baby at such a young age can feel such strong emotions and awareness of those around her dispels the myth that a baby will not be affected by things that happen in those very early weeks of life. (A website link for the video of the Still Face Experiment is included in the resource section.)

Throughout this book I will make many references to experts in the field of attachment – whether original theorists such as John Bowlby and Mary Ainsworth, or current workers in the field. The relevant books and resources are listed at the back of this book but I would encourage you to dig deeper into the works of:

- Dr Bruce Perry
- Dr Daniel Hughes
- Bryan Post
- Graham Music
- Louise Michelle Bomber.

Chapter 5

ATTACHMENT STYLES

There are four types of attachment styles that attachment theorists have categorised for us: one secure attachment and three disturbed or insecure attachment styles. It's important to note though that children, as with all of us, can't necessarily be labelled or pushed into pigeon-holes. I have however noticed in my own observations, and through the research of others, that children may have a tendency towards a style, or show patterns of a particular style. Some are very clearly one or another of these styles as they are essentially coping mechanisms to survive in the environments they have been forced to live in. For some children it is more difficult to identify which style they may have adopted but it's worth knowing what they are as it can give an indication to the way they behave.

SECURE ATTACHMENT (STYLE 1)

The first style of attachment is a secure attachment. This is when there is a healthy attachment between the child and caregiver. Most nurturing environments will mean the child grows and develops with a fairly secure attachment to others. They are able to build relationships, connect with the world around them and feel safe. These children will be able to leave their parent's side at the right time in their development to go and explore and come back to the safe parental base. Fortunately, many of us will have experienced such a childhood. There may be some aspects missing of course, as no parent is perfect, but there will be enough of a sense of security and love to be able to develop and function in a healthy way.

AVOIDANT ATTACHMENT (STYLE 2)

The main drive for a child with an avoidant attachment style is to not be noticed.

The strategy they have developed to keep safe in their environment is to stay below the radar – so they may come across as withdrawn, quiet and sometimes odd. They have learnt phrases to make you believe they are OK, but underneath they are hurting and very anxious.

An avoidant child's core belief is that he cannot trust an adult to meet his needs. He is often self-reliant and certainly does not want to ask for your help. He will appear very compliant and well behaved in class or in the group. His premise is that, if he cannot rely on adults to meet his needs, then he will make sure those needs are met – in whatever way possible!

There are times when he will 'help' even when you do not need or want him to.

An example of the intense self-reliance occurred very early on in our placement with our adopted children, when I took one of them to a birthday party. It was held at a soft play activity centre near to us and there were many parents and children milling around. Quite a few times I noticed that my child had food in his hand: a packet of crisps, a can of cola. I hadn't bought them so I wondered where they had come from.

As I continued to watch, I noticed that my child was scamming food from other parents. He obviously didn't feel that I would meet that need and so, instead of putting himself in the position of having to ask me and getting 'no' for an answer, he found a way to get what he needed himself.

An avoidant child will also be very reticent to let you know he is anxious. In the educational setting, he may pretend that he knows what is going on and what's expected of him but, deep down, he hasn't got a clue and is very anxious about that – and about letting you know.

The result of this, of course, is that the avoidant child does not progress in his learning as quickly as you would like. More often than not, he will understand something one day but the concept will have gone the next – he has not retained that information.

It was once described to me like the games you used to get at a fairground where the aliens randomly popped out of holes and you had to knock them down with a hammer. This is what an avoidant child feels many times: the thoughts, feelings and worries they have inside are constantly threatening to come out; the child works very hard to try to suppress those feelings and, as a result, is pre-occupied and exhausted from the emotional energy used to keep everything contained.

The children of course cannot articulate any of this to you – they are not aware of it themselves but you can guarantee they will not be concerned with times tables and fractions when they are working so hard to hide the nightmares or horrible feelings of fear and shame from their past.

Another analogy that I find helpful is if you imagine a portable radio – for an avoidant child their volume is turned down very low so that you have to get very close to them to hear what they are saying.

AMBIVALENT ATTACHMENT (STYLE 3)

In contrast, the aim of the ambivalent child is to be noticed; in fact you will know who he is because, if you don't, he's not doing his job properly.

If we think of our radio again his volume is turned up very high most of the time. He will be in your face, demanding attention constantly. He will be charming and helpful at times but aggressive and confrontational at other times. He tends to know everything that is going on: names, dates, places, who is missing – he doesn't miss a thing.

I heard once of a study undertaken in America with a group of high school students. Half of the group came from a difficult background and the other half were from a nurtured background. They were all asked to take part in a lesson and then they would be asked to answer a series of questions. Both sets of students sat through the lesson and both heard the same delivery. Both then answered the questions – some about the content of the lesson and the rest about what was happening in the room. What was the teacher wearing? How many students were there? What was happening outside in the playground? What was on the walls of the classroom?

The students from the nurtured background answered all the content questions perfectly but they could only answer a few of the observational questions. The disadvantaged students, however, answered very few of the content questions but they all knew what colour socks the teacher had on (Matthew, After Adoption Conference, Cardiff, 2012).

Ambivalent children will notice everything else that happens at school apart from the learning, as they are constantly on the lookout for changes or danger – things they may need to remember at some point – but they are so pre-occupied with this that they are inclined to miss what you are trying to teach them.

Additionally, ambivalent children will believe something is wrong if they are not being talked about by others. Hence, they will work very hard to be noticed, in a good way or otherwise – it doesn't matter to them.

The ambivalent child is like a container: the water you pour in is the amount of attention they need. The problem for these children is that their container has a leak in it – so however much attention you pour in, it is never enough.

DISORGANISED ATTACHMENT (STYLE 4)

The disorganised attachment style is as it sounds – very confused and disorganised.

This child hasn't yet developed a strategy to cope with his pain so he flips in and out of needing you, not wanting you, then needing you again. He can be quiet and withdrawn like the avoidant attachment style child. You have to work incredibly hard with his parents and carers to try and understand what's going on.

Going back to our radio for this child the volume is on but there is distortion and static on the line – you cannot really hear or understand what he is communicating at times.

As described earlier, the attachment styles are loosely linked to the kind of environment a child finds himself in. For a disorganised attachment style, the environment is likely to be a domestic violence type where the carer is both frightened and frightening.

Chapter 6

BRAIN DEVELOPMENT

An essential part of understanding children who have experienced trauma is an awareness of brain development. The impact of trauma for children is not only emotional but also physical. Once you can truly appreciate this, it will be much easier to understand their behaviour.

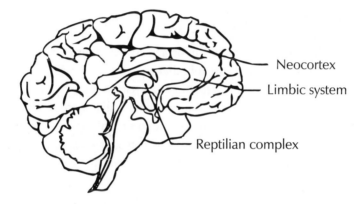

Neocortex

Limbic system

Reptilian complex

Figure 6.1 The triune brain.

The triune brain as illustrated in Figure 6.1 shows us three areas of the brain. The brain develops from the bottom up and inside to outside. The first part to develop is the back part of the brain known as the reptilian brain. This area of the brain is concerned with survival.

This is where the fight, flight, freeze mechanism lives and this is all we need when we're born – the instinct to survive.

As we grow and develop, the other two parts of the brain start to form, influenced by the repetitive interactions we experience. The next section (limbic system) is known as the emotional brain. This is where our feelings develop. Then, finally, the thinking brain (neocortex) develops. This is where all our logical thinking takes place – along with our reasoning, creativity, recognition of familiar faces, language and abstract thought. This is where most of us live most of the time – as you are reading this book, it is hoped that the frontal cortex (neocortex) of your brain is busy at work.

The interesting thing about the brain is that the reptilian brain and the thinking brain cannot both work at the same time: if the reptilian brain is fired up, the thinking brain is rendered inactive. This is for a very good reason. Imagine walking across a road and a car speeds around the corner towards you. You don't stop and use your neocortex, thinking to yourself, 'Right, what shall I do? Well, I could run to the pavement and hope I make it; I could lie down and hope the car swerves around me – or I could run back the way I came.' *No*, you don't have time to do that! Your thinking brain simply shuts down, your reptilian brain fires up and you run (or freeze).

But what happens for a child who has experienced early trauma? As his brain develops, the reptilian part of the brain is over-stimulated due to the stressful environment – it is hypersensitive and runs on overdrive, if you like. Whereas your reptilian brain fires up very occasionally (and you will remember when that happens as all reason disappears), for the child who has experienced early trauma, the reptilian part of the brain is on constant alert. As we've said, the thinking brain and the reptilian brain cannot work at the same time, which means that, for the child living in the reptilian part of the brain for the majority of the time, her frontal cortex is inactive. So, when she is asked to do her times tables, for example, and is over-anxious about what might happen to her if she doesn't get it right, she cannot access the part of the brain needed to do times tables.

It's not a case of 'won't do' – she simply can't!

This is why you may find that, with children such as this, they can do something one day, then the next day they can't. Something has changed to make the different parts of the brain fire up. The trick is to help them to calm down and feel safe so that the reptilian part of the brain becomes inactive and the frontal cortex can then become active.

Another aspect of our brain development is to do with connections in the brain called neurons. When we are born, we have more than ten billion brain cells (neurons), 50 per cent more than we need in later life. As we develop in those first two years of life, these cells start to make connections (synapses) through repetitive behaviour:

the consistent patterns of stimulation and interaction strengthen those synapses because we use them so much.

The synapses are the key functioning elements of the brain. They connect the cells and make sure communication is happening around the cells, which in turn send out the signals needed for our body to function in all the different ways it needs to.

These synapses periodically go through a pruning process: 'use it or lose it'. This process happens throughout childhood and the number of neurons increase and decrease at different times. Typically, the numbers increase up until adolescence and then decrease after adolescence.

The way this pruning process works is that, if a cell is not used regularly for any reason, its connection will just fall away.

> *This means that, for a child who isn't getting regular stimulation, touch, eye contact, smiles, nurture – all the things you need for healthy development – then those connections will fall away.*

Consider empathy, for example. When a child is not shown empathy – when they don't experience the dance of two-way communication that happens between adult and child – then that part of the brain doesn't wire properly. The child then finds empathy a very strange and difficult concept to understand and to actualise.

NEUROSEQUENTIAL MODEL

In Dr Bruce Perry's book, *The Boy Who Was Raised as a Dog* (Perry and Szalavitz 2006), he uses the various experiences he has had with different children to explain brain development with all its complexities, and the impact that has on a child.

One of the models he talks about is called the Neurosequential Model (see Figure 6.2). This model takes what we have discussed in the earlier part of this chapter to a deeper level. Dr Perry discovered through his research that children need:

> Patterned, repetitive experiences appropriate to their developmental needs, needs that reflect the age at which they'd missed important stimuli or had been traumatised, not their current chronological age. (Dr Bruce Perry, p.138)

When you look at the model in Figure 6.2, the picture shows the triune brain again developing upwards: first, the brainstem then the midbrain, the limbic system and, finally, the neocortex. This layer upon layer effect is how we develop many of our skills, emotions and abilities.

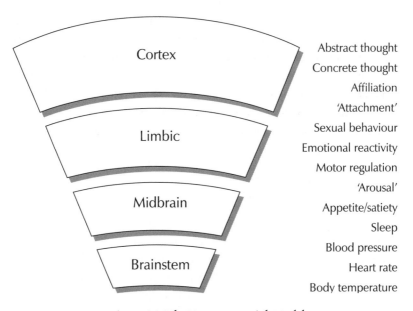

Figure 6.2 The Neurosequential Model.
Source: Dr Bruce Perry and Maia Szalavitz 2006, p.248

The list down the side of the model gives examples of areas where this applies. Let's take motor regulation, for example: rhythm and movement. This begins very early in a mother's womb. The baby feels the rhythm of Mum walking, and moving – and also her rhythmic heartbeat. Then, when baby is born, that rocking movement continues. When you watch a mother and baby, there's always movement involved. When you pick up a baby, you instinctively rock the child to and fro. Then, when the child starts to walk, there's rhythm and movement. Each experience builds on the one before. So the child learns rhythm. However, when this is neglected – the repetitive, patterned re-enforcement – the child struggles to develop in the area concerned. A child who has under-developed rhythm and movement, for example, begins to have problems with his gait, playing sport and dancing.

This important discovery helps us to understand that repetitive patterns of experiences are essential to a child's development. When she receives inconsistent care and stimulation, there are so many effects on physical development as well as on emotional development.

MIRROR NEURONS

There is another aspect to the relationship between carer and baby in those first few years. We have what's called *mirror neurons*, a set of nerve cells in the brain that respond to the behaviour of others. For example, when a mother smiles, baby smiles; when a mother points, baby points. This mirroring helps us as humans to develop the capacity for reciprocal relationship. When you see a mother and baby together you can see this mirroring in action: if there is a strong attachment and connection, the dance of mirroring is beautiful. Sometimes Mum leads, other times baby leads, but both are participating in the dance of relationship.

This dance of relationship is doing so much for the baby in that moment. Not only is there a bond being formed between both parties involved but the repetitive patterned activity stimulates the brain of the baby and the connections are made throughout the brain.

As mentioned earlier in the theorists chapter, Edward Tronick's Still Face Experiment demonstrates this perfectly. The baby responds to Mum and Mum responds to the baby; sometimes it's difficult to see who initiates the contact. When that is broken (the mother becomes vacant, distant or pre-occupied, for example), the impact on the child is striking. The baby is confused: 'What happened to my mirror?' This in turn throws baby into a panic state of desperately trying everything she can to reconnect.

It's heart-breaking to realise that this is what some children deal with daily in their early lives.

As we saw in the chapter on experiences that can contribute to trauma, there are many areas where parents sometimes unwittingly put their children in this position of being isolated and cut off from the dance of human interaction. Be it abuse, neglect, depression, pressures from elsewhere, pre-occupation with other children, personal grief or loss – all these things can break the connection children must have if they are to develop the skills needed to connect to others in the future.

Many of the birth parents of children in care, adopted or vulnerable, have come from the kind of environments we are talking about – they are the traumatised children now grown up. They then try to parent their own children when they have not got the capacity, understanding and resilience themselves to do it well enough. Of course, there are some who wilfully harm children and it is a complex issue (one we won't really go into in this book) but I would encourage you to be open to having a compassionate perspective, when needed, on the birth families involved with these children.

Chapter 7

SYMPTOMS OF
ATTACHMENT DIFFICULTIES

How can you tell if a child you are working with has attachment difficulties? Whether they fall into an avoidant, ambivalent or disorganised style of attachment, the symptoms may be very much the same. As you read through this list of symptoms, you may be saying to yourself, 'Well, all children do that', and you would be right. In some cases, all children will show similar behaviours. However, you need to be looking for the underlying root of the behaviour: does it come from fear and anxiety or pushing the boundaries in normal child development? Some of the symptoms are age-appropriate – so children having tantrums is, of course, very normal at the age of two, but not so at the age of ten!

It is also worth noting, before we look at the symptoms, that many other conditions have similar symptoms. Autism and Foetal Alcohol Syndrome, for example, present very similarly to attachment difficulties. These children may have been diagnosed with lots of other conditions such as ADHD (Attention Deficit Hyperactivity Disorder) and ODD (Oppositional Defiance Disorder).

If you know that a child is adopted or in the care system, it is very likely they will have some attachment difficulties to one degree or another, as the reasons children are taken into care these days are predominantly due to neglect and abuse.

The most common symptoms are as follows.

POOR SENSE OF IDENTITY

Children who have experienced trauma will very often not be secure in who they are as a person and they may struggle to think they are worthy of affection. This is for a number of reasons. At the core of their being they feel that they are bad, as mentioned earlier when looking at the disturbed attachment cycle. Also, in many cases, they don't know much about their early years – the memories and family history we can usually draw on.

These children will have a very blurred or difficult history and, in some cases, have blocked it out of their conscious mind completely.

You may very well see a child who does not know what he likes and doesn't like. He may change his behaviour and personality to fit in with whoever he is with, as he desperately wants to be liked and wants to fit in with others. He will also find some activities difficult, such as family trees and child growth and development projects, as he may not have any photos of himself as a baby and can't say who his smile is like, or who has the same eyes as him.

As these children get older, this poor sense of identity can cause problems as their bodies change and, as teenagers, they begin to find who they are. Most children have a strong enough base to fall back on as they explore the world and experiment in it. The children we're talking about, though, have very little to fall back on that will sustain them and bring them back to a safe place. Once they start to experiment, it can lead to all kinds of trouble, hence the terrible statistics of the outcomes for children in care:

- 67.8 per cent have special educational needs.

- Only 15.3 per cent achieve 5 or more GCSEs grades A*–C or equivalent.

- 6.2 per cent of looked after children aged between 10–17 have been convicted or subject to a final warning or reprimand

- 3.5 per cent have substance misuse problems.

- Twice as likely to be permanently excluded from school than other children.

- Nearly 3 times more likely to have a fixed term exclusion than other children.

- Around half of looked after children aged 5–16 are considered to be 'borderline' or 'cause for concern' in relation to emotional and behavioural health.

(Department for Education, 2013)

HYPER-VIGILANT (JUMPY AND ON EDGE)

As we've seen in the section on brain development, children living in the reptilian part of the brain most of the time – pre-occupied with survival – are constantly on edge, looking out for danger. Whilst we may not be able to understand how this would feel (that is, the intensity of the emotions involved), just imagine feeling constantly under threat. Those of you who may have experienced anything like a war will know the incredible pressure on your senses.

For these children, each change in circumstance, unexpected movement or funny look from a friend can send them into a state of panic and anxiety.

What you might see in these children is that they cannot concentrate on a task due to being hyper-alert to things around them. They may be able to access the front part of their brain one moment to do their times tables or understand an instruction you give them, but, the next minute, it's as if they had never learned the times tables or heard your instruction. They have flipped into the reptilian part of their brain and now cannot therefore access their thinking brain.

BECOMING OVER-EXCITED VERY EASILY

Children who have experienced early trauma have a tendency to become over-excited at the slightest thing – losing a pencil, someone ignoring them, not being first. As mentioned already, emotions are overwhelming for children – especially if they already have a higher base level of stress than others. If a baby is born with lots of cortisol from a stressed mother, for example, that baby is prone to feeling stress and becoming over-excited to the extent that they cannot then handle that level of arousal.

I see this many times in my own children. Activities that may appear to be OK for them such as free play – running around with their mates and chasing each other – can actually be too stimulating for them. If you watch carefully you can see that, for some children, this kind of uninhibited play causes them to lose control of their emotions and they then find it very difficult to come back down to a normal level.

UNDER-REACTION OR OVER-REACTION TO PAIN

Typically, children who have experienced early trauma don't react in the expected way to events. For example, pain is one area where they seem confused in how to respond. They can have a nasty fall with a painful graze on their legs and blood running down but show absolutely no response.

A few years ago I was called into school as one of my children had been swinging forward on their chair when the chair had slipped and they'd gone face down into the table. The interesting thing though was that they showed no reaction when it happened – just got up from the floor and sat down. It was only when someone said 'You have blood running down your face' that they realised the extent of what had happened – that actually they had quite a nasty cut on their face from grooves made in the table with a metal ruler. They still have a scar to this day! Once they had realised that it was all right to show pain and that they actually were in pain then the water works started and didn't stop for some time. On the flip side of this, the children concerned can over-react to a slight pin-prick on their finger, and it is as if their arm is about to fall off! It's very difficult to know if they really are in pain or not.

INAPPROPRIATE SEXUALISED BEHAVIOUR

Children may express things of a sexual nature that may alert you to the possibility that they may have experienced sexual abuse. However, there are a few reasons why a child may display inappropriate behaviour of this nature. One is that they may have witnessed or been party to something inappropriate and you may need to get other people involved and follow the safeguarding and disclosure policies you have. The other reason, though, may be that they have heard something in the playground – a new rude word that's made all their friends giggle. Most children will know not to do anything with that information – not to shout it out in class or in assembly.

However, a child who has come from a chaotic environment may not know these expectations or unspoken rules.

They may hear something and think 'What's that? Let's try it out.' They may shout out the new rude word in the classroom to see what reaction they get. It doesn't necessarily mean sexual abuse has taken place, but it is always a sensitive area that needs handling in a sensitive way.

INABILITY TO DESCRIBE THEIR FEELINGS

This, again, is something that we learn though our experiences with others in those early years: to know, understand and express our own feelings. Very often, children who have experienced early trauma will be able to point at pictures of faces and say 'happy', 'sad', 'confused' or 'surprised' – but to then internalise those feelings and say 'I am happy, sad, confused, surprised' they find remarkably difficult. It's no good asking them what they feel or why they did something as they may not be able to tell you.

Another thing that happens in childhood is that we learn how to express our feelings through the continual commentary of our parents – 'Oh, you're feeling hungry, aren't you?', 'No, it's cold, isn't it? Maybe you need another blanket', 'Ah, don't cry, Mummy's not going anywhere. You want Mummy, don't you?'

This commentary helps children to know and understand their feelings as they grow and can internalise these feelings themselves. If a baby hasn't had this natural commentary it can hinder his development of understanding emotions and feelings.

MEMORY AND ORGANISATIONAL DIFFICULTIES

Apparently, when we are stressed, we lose our short-term memory and become confused, hence the reason we might have the same argument over and over again with a loved one, expecting a different result, but, in that state of immense stress, we become confused.

> *For traumatised children, whose brains are pre-occupied and in a perpetual state of anxiety, being able to remember tasks and instructions – like the things that need to go in their book bags – is very difficult.*

Also if they have to relay instructions to others you have to assume they haven't relayed those instructions accurately as they may not have taken in the relevant details, or if they did take it in they very often cannot relay those instructions in an understandable way.

An example of this was a few months ago when one of my children was involved in a school production where they had a part to play and needed a costume. They came home and said, 'I need one of Dad's shirts – green' – to which I replied, 'Are you sure – your Dad's shirts will swamp you and I don't think he has a green shirt'. Then we had this very confusing discussion where the instructions changed from Dad's to big, from green to black, grey, blue, brown, from shirt to T-shirt – to which I was starting to get a tad frustrated. Anyway, eventually I thought I'd better call the school and get some clarification. When I was told what the instruction had been I could see what had happened. The instructions were 'Bring a big top/T-shirt, like your Dad's, of a dull colour like green, brown, grey or black.'

Now can you see the confusion for my child? They had heard parts of the instruction but it was far too vague and left too much to the child's imagination and assumed they could do abstract thinking.

MISTRUST IN RELATIONSHIPS

As described in the section on the disturbed attachment cycle (Chapter 3), children with a history of trauma have learnt not to trust others but to be self-reliant – mistrust is their default. They may seem like they trust you but, often, they have found ways to convince others they can trust; they learn the phrases and responses desired but, underneath, they are waiting for you to let them down – as people always have done in their world previously. Why would you be any different?

I've noticed recently that some of my children like to play trust games with me – they close their eyes as we hold hands and walk to the car. Sometimes they can keep their eyes closed, other times they can't, but I'm encouraged that they want to play these games with me and at least are showing some trust towards me.

This is harder in our educational settings however with staff member changes, transitions to different classes, primary to secondary – all the changes can mean if they do start to trust someone they have to start all over again with a new person. It must be very exhausting for them emotionally as it's such an effort to trust in the first place when it doesn't come naturally to you, and then to have to start all over again must be disheartening.

FRIENDSHIP DIFFICULTIES

Children who have experienced early trauma may appear very confident at first and make friends easily, but it is a superficial kind of friendship. The older they get, the more difficulties they find in sustaining friendships. This is for a number of reasons. First, they are not the same age emotionally as they are chronologically, due to the essential nurturing they have missed out on in early years. They will generally act like much younger children – and more so under stress. This means that the gap between them and their peers gets wider as they grow older – they may be 11 years old but still want to play role-play games and activities a five-year-old would play.

Second, they may not have had good role models who taught them the niceties of relationships, such as how to show empathy to others, how to prefer others, how to challenge and confront others when needed – all the nuances of relationships that, even as adults, we find difficult sometimes.

> *For children who have had little guidance – who don't understand emotions easily and who are coming from a place of mistrust – relationships are a minefield of anxiety.*

You may have noticed that vulnerable children gravitate towards each other. As much as you try to separate them they seem to want to be together even though the relationships are fraught with anxiety. This has always been confusing for me – the children that are mean to them, bully them and generally don't make great friends seem to be the ones they desperately want to be friends with. Some of this is due to how they feel at the core of their being – 'no-one would want to hang out with me so go for the ones who seem to be the same as me'. Also I think they instinctively feel different to other children their age who maybe haven't had the same experiences as them. To always feel inferior to others is not a nice place to be.

We have constant trials around relationships – I would say the majority of all our children's anxiety about school is based around fitting in with others.

LACK OF EMPATHY

Empathy is something we develop in those early few years of life through our interactions with others. Through mirroring, as mentioned earlier, we learn that others have a different point of view and can feel differently to us. For children who have missed those early experiences, empathy is a foreign language to them – one that needs lots of interpretation from others.

As an example of this, early on in our children's placement with us, one of them broke his arm on the trampoline. He, of course, screamed and then went very quiet as he was in shock – while the rest of the family were running around to try to handle this situation. Grandparents were called to come and sit for the other two whilst my husband and I took the injured one to hospital. While this running around was happening, one of the other children was distraught, as if it was happening to them – hysterically worrying about what had happened to their brother. Then the other child, who had been quiet during the proceedings, came up to me in the kitchen and asked quite sweetly, 'What's for dinner?' You can imagine I was dumbstruck! But the pain hadn't happened to him so why would he bother – nothing had changed for him!

OVER-FAMILIARITY WITH STRANGERS

This is a classic sign of a child with attachment difficulties and one that is very often misunderstood. These children will freely run up to people they don't know and hug them, kiss them or sit on their laps. They seem very confident and will go with anyone – which is not a good thing! There is no sense of 'stranger danger' for these children. People have come and gone in their lives: people they were told to trust having only just met them (social workers, foster carers, adoptive parents, doctors, teachers) lots of different people who they don't know but who are making decisions for their future.

Something I continually find curious is that, no matter how long a child stays in a place, they will always show this insecurity with new people. Very often, when they are introduced to people the parents may know but who are unknown to them, they will ignore the parent and stay glued to the new adult(s). It's as if they have a sense that these new people may be important to them and they need to make sure the newly met adults like them, in case they are going to live with them.

HEIGHTENED SENSE OF JUSTICE

This is something we see many times with our children. They can be very particular about the rules of a game, the fairness of discipline and the equality between adults and children, as well as between children.

Very often, children who have experienced early trauma will be very stringent about the rules.

If someone breaks the rules, they will let you know and will want to know what you are going to do to punish that person. They have a tendency to hold onto disappointment for hours and cannot reconcile the inequality and seemingly unfair way the world works. 'Why can the older children go on a trip and we can't?' 'Why can so and so have an extra biscuit and I can't?' 'You said last week I could have some time on the computer if I did my spellings and now you're saying there isn't time.'

This sense of unfairness and injustice can be a very strong hindrance to them being able to let things go and settle in a classroom, to be calm enough to learn.

LYING

Lying is a very common behaviour of traumatised children. In his book, *The Great Behaviour Breakdown*, Bryan Post (2009) gives a great explanation of lying and its link to stress:

> Everyone tells white lies at times, but why do we do it? You guessed it: stress. This stress causes the brain to have a fear reaction, which leads us to protect ourselves by telling the lie. So, can you understand why a child with a trauma history might be prone to lying? The child isn't trying to be manipulative or defiant. The lying is a result of stress. (Post 2009, p.57)

I have come to realise that, with lying, more may be going on for a child than trying to get themselves out of trouble. Recently, I knew of a child who was describing something that she did to her birth parents – a prank, an act of defiance – and whilst she was describing this, it became apparent to the person listening that she was recounting a scene from a film, namely *Matilda*. The child was adamant, though, that it was what she actually did. Once she'd finished describing the prank and, as the person talked to the child, it became clear that it was what the child would have liked to have done to her parents – what she wanted to do to them if she could!

She was so absolutely positive that it was the truth that, if you hadn't known the scene from the film, you would have believed her.

So, it's not always that they are telling bare-faced lies – it's a bit more complicated sometimes. It could be what they want to do, or what they really believe happened. Perspective is a strange concept and sometimes it's hard to distinguish between fact and fiction.

STEALING

This shows up many times for children with a history of early trauma. In early years at school, for example, they may steal something from home to give to friends. They may not know the worth of the item and that doesn't really matter – its purpose is to win affection from others and buy friends. As children grow older, though, this tendency to steal can create a great problem for them – and for you trying to work with them.

In, *The Great Behaviour Breakdown*, Post lumps stealing and self-mutilation together in a single chapter. The reason for this, he says, is that 'both are addictive behaviours'. The reason we need addictions – which may be coffee or chocolate for you and me – is that it helps us to manage our internal dysregulation: 'it's an external attempt to soothe an internal state', says Post (2009, p.69). The trick is to try to understand the stress related to the time and place of the child's stealing – and then help him manage that stress so that he doesn't feel the need to steal.

DIFFICULTIES WITH EYE CONTACT AND TOUCH

Eye contact is something we seem to believe is a sign of respect – especially from a child when we're telling him off. If he is not looking directly into our eyes, we assume he is not listening or he is not contrite and humble enough. However, for the children we're talking about in this book, forcing them to look into your eyes, especially under stressful circumstances, is too much for them to bear.

Think back to what their primary belief about themselves is: that *they* are bad – at the very core of their being, they feel dirty and worthless. When you then get that child to look you in the eyes, that intense feeling of someone seeing deep inside of you makes him feel very vulnerable – he thinks you can see that ugly part of him that he's worked so hard to hide.

Touch can also be a difficult area for these children: they may flinch when you go near them or, alternatively, they may shower you with inappropriate affection. Both are signs of attachment difficulties.

LACK OF CAUSE-AND-EFFECT THINKING

A lot of the games we play when we're toddlers are about cause and effect: you push this button and up pops the rabbit; you twist this lever and a noise comes out. The way we interact with a baby is very much about cause and effect: if I smile at Mummy she smiles back. It helps us to understand that there's a consequence to everything we do.

Think about children who have had a difficult start, whether through neglect (where there wasn't much stimulation and those games of peek-a-boo) or abuse (where a child received a negative reaction for so much of what they did). When these things happen, the cause-and-effect process in their brains becomes confused.

In later life, children who have experienced such neglect or abuse don't understand that if they hit someone there is a consequence, and that if they throw a ball at a window, the window might break.

You will see this lack of cause-and-effect thinking in the way some children seem to have no impulse control. Most of us, when we have an urge to do something potentially hazardous such as bungee jumping, stop and think about the consequences and the risks and then decide whether or not we want to actually undertake the activity. For traumatised children, the middle part of the thinking process is simply missed out: 'I hate Billy for what he just did' – then, bang, a punch on his nose.

INABILITY TO COPE WITH CHANGE OR TRANSITION

This is a common symptom of attachment difficulties. Such a child finds it almost impossible to cope with unplanned and unexpected change – and often with planned and expected change as well! This inability may manifest itself in tantrums, running away, defiance or refusal to move on to a new activity. It can be as simple as stopping a game they are enjoying to move onto another game they will probably enjoy just as much. To them all they feel is that the game they love is going to end – and they may never be allowed to play that game again.

DISASSOCIATION (TUNING OUT)

Disassociation occurs when a child reaches such a high state of stress that he zones out: he becomes disconnected with the world around him.

> *A child I know describes this feeling as like being on the end of a kite – not a nice, excited flying-in-the-air feeling, but a scary, out-of-control feeling.*

Children with trauma are often mistakenly tested for epilepsy as this 'tuning out' can look very much like petit mal seizures commonly experienced by those suffering with epilepsy.

POOR ATTENTION AND LISTENING SKILLS

Thinking back to the chapter on brain development, you will recall that there are physical reasons why a child who has experienced trauma may find concentration difficult. The hyper-vigilance of living in the reptilian part of the brain, for example, means the child has no space or energy left to listen to instructions or, indeed, learn times tables. Neither can he take in the several pieces of information we are inclined to give all at once. For my own children, I have to give them bite-sized chunks of instruction: 'Go and brush your teeth and then come back here.' Then, 'Now put your shoes on and sit down.' Telling them to just get ready to go out is not explicit enough because they forget what is actually involved in getting ready.

ERRATIC PROGRESSION IN LEARNING

When considering other forms of special needs such as autism, the progress that's made is very small but, nevertheless, steady. For children with attachment difficulties, on the other hand, that progression can be up and down from one day to the next and even from one moment to the next. This can be very frustrating and difficult to understand: you think you're moving on one day, only to find that the child has totally forgotten what they learnt the next.

This apparent forgetfulness in learning can be explained by the state that the child is in at a moment in time. Can they access the frontal cortex of their brain, for example? Are their basic needs being met (such as hunger) so that they can relax and concentrate on learning?

DIFFICULTIES WITH SPEECH AND LANGUAGE, FINE AND GROSS MOTOR SKILLS

All the skills we learn in those very early years will most likely be impaired in some way if a child has a history of early trauma: the child may experience difficulty in sports or writing; their speech may be delayed or a stammer develop; they may be delayed in their toileting. All these outward difficulties can be signs of early trauma.

DON'T RESPOND TO REWARDS AND SANCTIONS

This one has created much discussion in the workshops I've delivered to many education professionals. Behaviour modification techniques often do not work in the long term for these children. Sticker charts, sliding scale reward charts, certificates and praise assemblies can all add to the anxiety for these children. Why is this?

Well, think again about what they believe about their worth – that they are bad, naughty, unworthy children. When you then say, 'Wow, Sally, you did really well there. Here's a sticker!', their reaction might be to take the sticker and then go and punch another child, leaving you perplexed. Two things are happening here for the child: first, she doesn't believe you – she is convinced she is bad and will prove this to you by doing something 'bad' – and, second, because she doesn't believe you she thinks you are a liar and therefore untrustworthy, which erodes the trust you've started to build up with her.

We need to move away from behaviour modification and towards helping the child manage his stress and anxiety. Behaviour is just a way of communicating a need for these children. If they are hitting others or they are sullen and withdrawn, it is for a reason. We need to help them find that reason and help them make sense of it.

There's another thing that can happen in terms of rewards when it comes to charts on a wall. There are many around in classrooms these days that are some variation of a sliding scale. For example, everyone starts the day in the green and then as the day progresses they slide through amber if they're not doing well and then end up in red.

For the children we're talking about here (and actually probably most children, I'd hasten to add), this has a negative impact for two reasons. First, they may say to themselves, 'What's the point? I'm always going to end up in red because I'm so rubbish, so I might as well not bother.' Second, if they have an ambivalent style of attachment (attention-needing), then to be in the red is a good thing – they get more attention in the red area!

Part 2

GUIDING PRINCIPLES

Now that we've looked at the impact of trauma on children, both physically and emotionally, Part 2 is about looking at ways to help the ones in the settings you are in. I truly believe that 80 per cent of making a difference to these hard-to-reach children is about understanding what is going on for them. Being able to see them, not as 'naughty' children, but as scared, anxious children, whose behaviour is communicating their need to you, will revolutionise the way you approach them.

So, in this next part, we will take a further look at some guiding principles when working with these children in schools, which can also be applied by readers working with children in a more unstructured environment, such as youth groups, churches and children's clubs, for example. Having a set of principles will help you when looking at your programmes and working out how to really support these children and get them engaged. Also, for those in schools, being able to have some guiding principles that you can adapt and apply to your school environment will help you to make sure you can change something about your practice that will have a huge impact on the children and your relationship with them.

Chapter 8

GUIDING PRINCIPLE 1: RELATIONSHIPS OVER PROGRAMMES

Relationships are key to all children, but especially to children who have already encountered problems in relationships and have therefore experienced early trauma.

People have let them down, have hurt them, have not protected them and have not been able to meet their needs. Therefore, the future relationships they have with parents or carers and others with whom they come into contact are vitally important.

This means that when you're planning activities for these children, whether in an educational setting or as a recreational focus, relationships are paramount. The more you can build trust in your interactions with these children, the more they will be able to access what you want them to take on board.

On the subject of relationships, there is a very useful methodology created by Dr Dan Hughes, a child psychologist from America, that I have found invaluable with my own children and which I believe is a simple enough model to apply to how you relate to children in any setting.

He calls this model PACE: *Playful, Accepting, Curious, Empathic.*

PLAYFULNESS

First, it is important to realise that children who have experienced early trauma have lived in chaotic environments where little or no fun and laughter would be heard. If it was, it may have been cruel, unpredictable and inappropriate. Many children from these environments then find it very difficult to behave the way you would expect them to.

They need help in understanding play and laughter and the rules involved.

When you can approach a troubled child with a playful attitude, it takes away some of the anxiety and the fear of stern, harsh responses. As we've mentioned previously, these children feel terrible about themselves and expect to be in trouble and told off. So, when their defiance is met with play, it can defuse an explosive situation.

Nancy Thomas, another American expert in attachment, uses this approach with her children. She will hide sweets in her socks, for example, so that the children can find them. It is a different way of handling situations and it can feel that you are rewarding difficult behaviour, but some children just need a different approach – they have been punished more than enough in their short lives. They need a thoroughly radical approach, a way to get out of their reptilian brains and into a space of play and freedom.

ACCEPTING

Traumatised children have felt rejected and abandoned in many ways throughout their lives. If they have been adopted, they will have lost at least two sets of very influential people in their lives – their birth parents and their foster carers. Feeling acceptance can be difficult for any child, but, for children who've experienced trauma, they feel the total opposite: a great sense of shame – the belief that they are wrong, bad and unworthy. Helping them to feel accepted will contribute significantly to their healing.

The problem is that most of our education environments are not geared for acceptance of these children. They will invariably have difficulties with learning, attention and concentration, fine motor skills and forming and maintaining relationships. In fact, all the things that might make children feel they 'fit in' are areas of struggle for them.

It's essential, then, to find ways to help them feel accepted and included, whatever their behaviour may be.

Being able to handle them and their behaviour is important for them to know – if you can't handle them, they receive the powerful message, albeit the wrong message, that they are so awful that no-one can be around them.

The other area of acceptance is to be able to accept the child's inner world, as Dr Dan Hughes and Kim Golding say in their brilliant book, *Creating Loving Attachments*:

> Acceptance...means becoming aware of and understanding the other's thoughts, feelings, wishes, beliefs – that is, her inner life – without trying to change it. You simply experience what her experience is and understand it as it is, not as you might want it to be. There are no strings attached with acceptance. You are open to her inner life. You deepen your experience of her experience, rather than focus on trying to influence it... Only behaviour is evaluated, not her inner life. (Hughes and Golding 2012, p.87)

Being able to truly accept a child's inner thoughts, feelings and intentions may be very difficult for the adult but very empowering for the child. We all know that when we feel someone accepts us, warts and all, we are then able to change our inner world ourselves through a process of acceptance and then transformation. If we deny our true feelings, it is then incredibly difficult to truly change.

The same is true for children who've experienced trauma: their dark and sometimes nasty thoughts and feelings are very real; they need others to see that and to accept that those feelings are part of their experience in order for the child to be able to integrate those feelings and start to heal.

CURIOSITY

I love this one. Approach these vulnerable children with an attitude of curiosity. What is it that drives them? What's important in their life? How can you get to the core of who they are and bring out the best in them?

Being curious means you won't judge them so quickly. You can ask more questions of them – you are curious to know more about them. Asking questions is the best way to stay curious and let them know they are interesting to you. For example, instead of asking 'Why did you do that?', which implies it was a wrong or even stupid thing to do, a better question might be 'I wonder what was important about doing that?' or 'How did it make you feel when you did that?' See the difference? There's no judgement – just curiosity.

Staying curious helps you to stay accepting of their inner world.

Once you slip into judgement, it's very hard to accept someone's inner world. Curiosity also helps you to keep calm yourself. If a child is behaving in an aggressive manner, for example, then staying curious and wondering what may be going on inside for the child helps you to keep yourself regulated. It's not about you – it's about them!

EMPATHY

This one, again, is essential. To be able to see things from a child's point of view really makes the difference in how she feels. People often pity adopted children or those in care. They feel sorry for how their lives have turned out but those children need more than that. They need your empathy – the ability to understand and share the feelings of another (says the Oxford English Dictionary).

When someone really understands you, it creates a strong connection. For traumatised children especially, being able to trust an adult who seems to really 'get' them will be an amazing and transformational experience for them.

We will look closer at empathy in a further chapter when we look at specific areas of difficulty for these children. However, for those working with children who have experienced trauma, it is important to understand your own empathy journey from childhood: empathy develops very early in life through those first interactions with adults. Your ability to empathise as an adult will depend largely on how you were shown empathy as a child – which can make this part of PACE a difficult one for you.

PACE is a powerful approach to use with children who are vulnerable and need handling differently. When you're thinking about programmes, remember relationship is key and time and opportunity for building relationships needs to be built in. The approach we take to children with a history of trauma needs playfulness, acceptance, curiosity and empathy.

Chapter 9

GUIDING PRINCIPLE 2: EMOTIONAL AGE OVER CHRONOLOGICAL AGE

When thinking about children who have experienced early trauma, how do you benchmark them against others in their age range? Maybe you expect them to act like a seven-year-old, whatever that means, because that is their age – when, actually, their emotional age is more like that of a four-year-old.

The guiding principle here is about understanding the emotional age of children in the learning environment or wherever you come into contact with them. When you can understand and really 'get' that they are not operating at their chronological age, it makes learning easier for them, and also for you, as someone trying to help them to learn or to join in certain activities.

Children who miss out on essential early nurturing experiences in safe relationships may be functioning at a very immature level emotionally.

They may not have reached the stage of 'mutual play' (Winnicott 1971, p.68), which is necessary for learning and being able to see things from another's point of view.

There will be many occasions when such children will not be able to do things expected of others their age. As you've already seen in Part 1, their brain development is delayed and even damaged, to the extent that they live more in the primitive part of the brain – the survival instincts – than in the logical, reasoning, emotional regulation and reflective part of the brain. The processing skills involved in learning, therefore, are just not there sometimes, and, if they are, it will need lots of emotional regulation to enable the child to access them.

Research has shown that there is a strong link between our cognitive ability and our emotional development. Our first experiences of learning as a human are in those very early stages of infancy through the relationship with our primary caregiver. What that relationship was like, whether it was a trusting, strong, safe relationship of stimulation or otherwise, significantly affects our future relationships and our ability to learn.

Bowlby (cited in Wallen 2007, p.26) talks of an 'internal working model' – how a child feels about himself in the world based on interaction with his mother. When that relationship has been healthy and all secure attachments made, the child's sense of identity and worth develops. The child then uses that safe base from which to go and explore the world: his 'internal working model' is one of a lovable, significant person in relation to an adult who loves and is interested in him. In his future, this model is transferred to his teacher or helper, who may be considered an 'educational attachment figure' (Barrett and Trevitt 1991, p.198).

This, of course, can happen in all aspects of life – not just in education settings, but in youth clubs and scout groups, too; any place, in fact, where the child spends time and has the potential to form relationships. This puts pressure on the teacher or helper, especially if you do not understand this complex dynamic. Without understanding, there may be confusion about behaviours and the differences between children of the same chronological age. 'Why does Billy always want to draw attention to himself?' 'Why can't Sally just get on and play nicely with others?' 'What can I do to engage Michael in sharing a game?'

Knowing that a child may not have reached a certain developmental stage is helpful. Benchmarking can create difficulties for children, as they will feel the pressure and anxiety associated with having to 'perform' in a certain way. We all know that having to perform can be incredibly stressful; children who have experienced trauma can often come to school or a club in a heightened emotional state already. It will take them time to regulate to the calm state where they can listen and learn.

Research, around helping children with early trauma to heal, talks about allowing them to experience the earlier stages of development again – or for the first time, in many cases. They may have never known how to share, how to listen to others, how to empathise and how to use their imagination in play. Imagine a child who has never been played with in those early years; then to be expected to know the rules of play, how to interact with others and what is acceptable would be near impossible.

Of course, we're not saying that as someone in an educational setting you will be able to offer the earlier stages of emotional development that children may need, in terms of nurturing and bonding to a primary caregiver. What you can do, however, is understand where they are at and modify activities and tasks to their emotional level. Of course there are targets to be met, but how great would it be to be able to provide opportunities for children that could encourage them to develop emotionally, whilst not making them feel 'abnormal' compared to their peers?

There are two ways you can help children with this. One is to create opportunities for them to fill in the gaps they may have missed, but in an appropriate way. For example, in schools, as children get older, we give them tasks with younger children to give them a sense of responsibility. For the children we're looking at, these tasks can also help them to catch up on missed early experiences essential for their emotional development. For example, when they are in later years in Primary School they do playground duty for the early years, it gives them the chance to run around and skip and play like a five-year-old without their peers looking at them as if they have gone mad. Playground duty, supervised mentoring of younger children, reading to younger children, playing with younger children – these tasks all help the traumatised child to re-connect to those essential stages in emotional development.

The other area where you can help is when a child regresses to a younger emotional age due to stress: meet the child at that age. We all apparently regress under stress but, for most of us, it is hoped that will only be a few years and we readjust very quickly. A 15-year-old child who has experienced early trauma, however, can regress to the emotional age of a five-year-old under stress. What we are inclined to do in these circumstances is attempt to persuade the child to 'act their age'. We may not say those precise words but instead use pacifiers like 'Oh, it's not that difficult – someone of your age should be able to do that no problem.' Or 'Come on, look – all the other ten-year-olds can do this – have a go.' It just gives the message that they need to grow up.

So what would you do with a five-year-old (even though the child in front of you kicking and screaming is actually ten)? Just approach him as you would a five-year-old. Of course, you have to be mindful of the guidelines in your setting but you may decide to do some colouring together to help him calm down, tell the child a story, read to him or give him a hug and say 'Yes, it does hurt, it is difficult to lose a pencil.' Meet the child where he is at.

Chapter 10

GUIDING PRINCIPLE 3: STRUCTURE OVER CHAOS

The 'free time' periods we give children in educational or recreational settings can, in fact, be 'fear time' for vulnerable children. With no planned activities, they have to find things to do and deal with relationships with others – it is simply an opportunity to wind themselves into a frenzy of running around and bashing into people and things. Basically, what we as adults consider to be a time when children can just play, and do what they want, can in fact be very stressful for the most vulnerable children.

> For children who have lived in a chaotic environment, and may still be living in that chaos, unstructured time can bring on more anxiety and stress, resulting in difficult behaviour – either during that free time or when we then try and move them onto a quieter activity.

In a later chapter we will look more closely at self-regulation but we have already mentioned that, for some of the children concerned, their resting heart rate is faster and their stress level higher than that of other children. It therefore doesn't take much for their emotions to spiral out of control – but it takes a lot of effort to bring them down again.

Whenever you think of your environment and especially the activities you do with children, consider how you can create more structure for the most vulnerable. Think of a metal box with a velvet lining. Those children need to have strong, solid boundaries and clear structure – but with the softness of the PACE approach we looked at earlier. Both are vitally important: the strong, clear structure hand in hand with the soft, empathic approach.

Of course, children who have experienced early trauma can run around and play games like others – and we want to encourage that – but they need to have close supervision, clear instructions and unambiguous rules to enable safe play. In youth clubs, for example, having enough adults to be able to pay close attention to the most vulnerable children is essential. They may look as if they are OK and even tell you so, but be mindful that they need to know you are there and are able to step in if needed.

My own children will often play well together, but, if I am in their view, they know that there is someone watching them and concerned enough to give them the safety and structure they need. So, at times, I may just need to say, 'That's enough of that game now; what about trying…'

There's another element of this concept of 'structure over chaos' that I find fascinating: due to their early traumatic experiences, if such vulnerable children find things are too calm for them, they will sometimes push for chaos: they will do things to create the atmosphere that is comfortable and 'normal' for them; they will push your buttons to see if you will shout and to see if they can break the order and stability you are trying to maintain. Even though they hate the chaos because it scares them, it's a more familiar place for them, so they will do whatever it takes to recreate that environment. Just be mindful of this!

Chapter 11

GUIDING PRINCIPLE 4: TIME IN OVER TIME OUT

Theories and techniques about parenting have abounded over the years. Our thoughts, attitudes and understanding around leaving a baby to cry, for example, have dramatically changed as we've learnt the impact of this on the child. 'Spare the rod and spoil the child', 'a child should be seen and not heard' and many more sayings show us just how times have changed. One of the most prevalent techniques over the years was brought to the masses by Supernanny: the 'time out' sanction. This has been around for years but it has grown in popularity since Supernanny Jo Frost advocated it in her TV shows.

The idea is that, if a child misbehaves, he is sent to a 'time out' spot: a chair, a step, a corner of the room, somewhere suitable for him to be alone for a short while. He stays there for one minute of each year of his life – so five minutes for a five-year-old, ten minutes for a ten-year-old. If he comes away from the area too soon, the parent or carer puts him back on the spot and the timer starts again. Once the time is up, the child is then asked to apologise for his behaviour, the parent hugs him and reconciles and then they both move on.

Of course we don't use that exact technique in our schools and other environments outside the home but in my travels around schools, I've come to see that we do a variation of the naughty chair: the reflection spot, the carpet, the mat, a chair in the corner, the cooler or quiet room and, in some schools, children are even sent to stand outside the classroom or, worse, outside the head teacher's office.

Whilst I don't wish to make a specific statement about this technique for all children, it is not helpful for children who have experienced trauma and can actually be quite damaging.

Think back to our attachment cycle: for a child who has experienced a disturbed attachment cycle, the core belief that he holds of himself is that *he* is bad. When he then does something unacceptable to us as adults, how we respond affirms the core of what he already believes. For example, if he is running around in class and we send him to 'time out' – wanting him to know that what he has done is bad – the message he actually receives is that *he* is bad: another instance of rejection and abandonment.

Another aspect to always keep in mind with such children is that their emotions are powerful and overwhelming. If you have ever struggled with feelings of grief, anger and despair, you will know that they can be all-consuming. For a six-year-old who has already experienced immense rejection, loss and abuse – who is constantly living in that reptilian part of the brain – those feelings of anger and frustration can seem overpowering to him and he can feel that he is suffocating under the pressure of them. It sounds dramatic, I know, but, to the child, it really does feel like a matter of life or death in that moment.

I've also been confronted with another realisation recently with one of my own children: the fear that vulnerable children have that we as adults cannot cope with their emotions. Because their behaviour can be so challenging and difficult, they internalise that to mean that *they* are challenging and difficult – everything about them: their inner world of thoughts, feelings, hopes, wishes, intentions, motivations – everything.

> *The message the child receives is: if adults can't even cope with me, what hope do I have of controlling my emotions and being able to function normally?*

So, let's get back to our guiding principle on 'time out'. There are, in fact, two types of time out. The first is the one I've described above, which is used as a behaviour modification technique. The second, though, is about *taking yourself* to time out – giving yourself space to work through your feelings. A child who has experienced early trauma will need help to recognise for themselves that they need this kind of time out. As adults, we certainly need to take ourselves out of situations from time to time to calm down, think and assess circumstances and our responses to them. We may do that through taking a walk, having a cup of tea, watching TV, chatting to a friend – we have many ways of regulating our emotions. In our educational settings, we can teach children to do that for themselves – to be able to feel when they are becoming upset and angry and take a walk, read a book or step out of an activity. They are all great things to encourage children to do.

However, back to our time out in the Supernanny sense: instead of sending a child away from you to a 'naughty' step, a highly recommended strategy by many experts in this field is *time in* instead of *time out*. Louise Bomber, in her book *Inside I'm Hurting* (2007), talks about this approach and gives practical ways of using time out in a good sense and also how to use time in.

HOW DOES 'TIME IN' WORK?

When you can see a child becoming frustrated or dysregulated, pre-empt his anxiety and bring him close to a trusted adult. They want to be close to people to feel safe – especially when their feelings are so powerfully negative. So you can say, 'Sally, why don't you come and help me sort out these books?' or 'Tom, can you come and help me colour this page?' and 'Jane, why don't you help Miss Jones to tidy the toys?' The idea is that you bring the child towards you before they get to the stage of having to be removed from other children because they are a danger to themselves or others.

This technique is often hard for us to understand if we feel we have to let the child know he has done something wrong, but the reason he behaves in a certain way is due to fear and anxiety not 'naughtiness'.

One example of this is of a little girl in pre-school – Julie. At the end of the day, the routine in this pre-school was for all the children to go to their pegs to get their things to go home. The pre-school staff were aware of Julie's anxieties around the other children, and that she often felt frightened by lots of noise and chaos. One day, at the end of the school day, the children were all sent at the same time to get their things. Julie's peg was in the middle of all the pegs. Julie is a smaller child than her peers and so she started to push her way through the crowd of pre-schoolers. As her anxiety built up, she clawed her way near to her peg and then started to pull the hair of the child in front of her peg. This, of course, got the attention of the staff and, as a result, Julie was told off and her parent brought into the school to talk about her behaviour.

Let's look at that again: from what you know so far about vulnerable children, what is going on for Julie? She is probably already anxious about home time – wanting to go back to where she feels some security; she struggles with communicating and expressing her needs so doesn't say anything to the other children or adults about not being able to reach her peg.

Once in the chaos of lots of arms and legs and noise and pushing, she resorts to the only thing she feels she can do – using force to get what she needs. She is then punished for that, which reinforces the signal that she is a bad girl, someone who can't control herself – and so she feels ashamed again!

This is a simple example of a stressful situation that could have been avoided for Julie – and the children she hurt in the process. The staff could have easily held Julie back for five minutes with a small job: 'Come and help me sort these toys out, Julie.' After the noise of the other children had abated, she could have then calmly got her things before leaving to meet her mum.

Chapter 12

GUIDING PRINCIPLE 5: SENSORY LESS OVER SENSORY MORE

I am forever amazed at how much stimulation children seem to need these days. I'm showing my age here but, when I was a child, we didn't have PlayStations and DSs; we spent our days playing outside from breakfast until tea-time. The culture is very different now for our children. Everywhere you look is about stimulation (films, adverts, music) – very much an 'entertain me now' culture.

Of course progress is a good thing and technology has changed the way we live, but for children who have a very busy and chaotic mind, lots of sensory stimulation can be a negative thing.

Programmes for young people now tend to be fast paced: activities have to be punchy with lots of colour, music and variety. Even within our schools, we now have many different ways to engage children in their learning and it is a good thing that we are able to help children in this way – not just by listening to the teacher. However, as we know, traumatised children's senses are very often working overtime. Smells, sounds, taste, sights and touch – any of the senses can be triggered to take them back to their early traumas.

The sense of smell, in particular, is apparently the only sense that links directly to the emotional part of our brains. Children who have been taken from their abusive or neglectful environments as babies may not have cognitive memories, but their senses have memories – they may remember smells, sounds and feelings.

Going back to our first guiding principle of relationships over programmes, you will recall that vulnerable children do not need more stimulation – they need more connections with trusted adults and peers. I often advise schools I work with about being mindful of the impact of over-stimulation on vulnerable children. It may, in fact, be better to keep them out of the activities to protect them from the fear and anxiety generated by that activity. School trips to theme parks are an example: whilst they are a great experience and most children will want to go, children who find regulating their emotions difficult will find being on a roller coaster of overpowering, overwhelming emotions all day long just too much for them to handle and the result will be difficult behaviour – or even meltdown.

Another time of year when this principle is of particular significance is at Christmas. The change in routine and a continual round of exciting activities makes for a very difficult month for vulnerable children. Actually keeping things quiet and low key is much more desirable for them.

So when you are considering suitable activities for children who have experienced early trauma, think about 'sensory less' – quiet and peaceful, small groups, more adult contact – instead of the fast-paced, noisy, highly stimulating activities that other children may enjoy. Actually, all our children would benefit from learning how to be quiet and how to entertain themselves instead of being continually entertained by machines or other people.

Part 3

AREAS OF CONCERN

In this next part, we will delve deeper into some specific areas that children who have experienced trauma find particularly challenging. There will be explanations of what the areas are, why they are a problem for such children and some strategies for helping them in these areas. Of course, the list is not exhaustive: we could fill many books on the complex issues children face, but these are the ones I have had personal experience with in my own family and also from other families I know.

Chapter 13

TOXIC SHAME

Shame is not guilt. It isn't that feeling when you know you've done something wrong and you wish you could take it back. Shame is a deeper feeling: it's a powerful emotion that's meant to motivate us to undertake a desired behaviour. We need shame. Its function is to help us stop doing the things that aren't good for us and to start doing things that are.

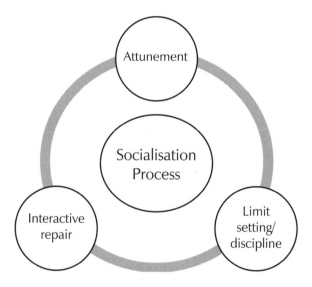

Figure 13.1 Usual socialisation process.

The socialisation process, shown as a cycle in Figure 13.1, starts with *attunement* – that is, the relationship between the child and parent, carer, teacher, whoever he or she might be. This is the dance we covered earlier, where there is trust and safety. Then events take place and the adult sets *limits* or *boundaries*. For example, if a child runs into the road, the adult shouts after the child, pulls him back if close enough, and then chastises him for running into the road.

That feeling the child feels at that moment of chastisement is shame. He knows he's done something wrong and he *feels* awful about it – and he doesn't like that feeling. Following the setting of boundaries, the cycle continues with *interactive repair*, in other words, the adult talks to the child about why he was told off, hugs him, comforts him and helps the feeling of shame go away.

What happens as a result of this scenario is the child knows that horrible feeling of shame was just that – horrible. He doesn't want to experience that again so the next time he is by a road, he thinks twice about running into the road. That's what shame is there for. Initially shame is big; over time, through repetition of this process, shame gets smaller and guilt begins to develop – that is, the ability to see what I have done to someone else and want to make it right with that person.

Whilst researching this, I was surprised to discover that, according to Dr Daniel Sonkin:

> no-one is perfect – even for the most secure parents, they are only 30% attuned – but they know how to repair mis-attunements (2009.)

That's the key: being able to repair the relationship once that limit-setting or discipline has taken place.

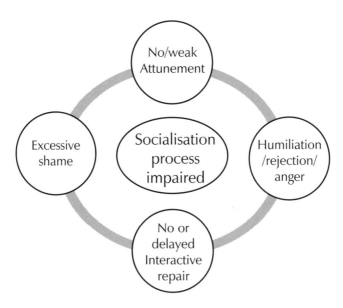

Figure 13.2 Impaired socialisation process.

Figure 13.2 shows what happens when that socialisation process is impaired. To start with, the attunement between the adult and child may not be there at all or very weak. Imagine a child in a domestic violence type of environment. The adult may be angry, confused and anxious themselves – pre-occupied with keeping themselves safe. The connection between adult and child will be fragmented, if there at all.

Within such a cycle, the chastisement comes more in the form of humiliation, rejection and anger, sometimes on an on-going basis. For example, a child may be shouted at for needing the toilet, or expressing feelings, being hungry and wanting attention and affection. This creates fear, rage and self-hatred – very powerful overwhelming emotions. The child starts to feel that *he* is bad – not what he is doing or is asking for.

When in this place, shame loses its effectiveness and becomes toxic. Once the child enters that state of shame, there is either very little repair, no repair or very delayed repair, which leads to an inability to self-soothe, to a feeling of isolation and to an expression of displaced anger towards others.

The child can then become stuck in a state of excessive shame. This becomes debilitating and can lead to chronic anger and controlling behaviour. The child has the sense that nothing is ever good enough – that they are not good enough. They become trapped in a prison of shame, which affects their ability to regulate emotions, control their impulses and think rationally.

As we talked about earlier in the usual socialisation process, what also happens is that shame moves to guilt as children understand that they impact on others. However, those children who are stuck in that toxic shame place do not move on to fully understand guilt. Shame remains huge and they don't develop the ability to feel that they need to make something right that they have done to someone else. Many times with my children they will say sorry because they are learning that process without actually first understanding that they have done anything to be sorry about.

Another sign that a child has experienced toxic shame is their hypersensitivity to any kind of criticism. You may just say, 'Oh, you could have been a bit neater with that handwriting, Billy', and he explodes with unexpected and uncontrollable rage.

Other manifestations of toxic shame include running and hiding, lying, controlling people and situations, blaming and punishing others

– or the inability to experience joy, peace, humour, uninhibited play and spontaneity.

An example of such toxic shame is explained in a book called Shame and Guilt by Jane Middleton-Moz (1990). She talks a little about her own experience of growing up:

> I was a child ashamed of feeling unhappiness. I was ashamed of tears, of being sick, of making a mistake or of having needs. Additionally, I was ashamed of feeling pride in myself. I questioned, why would a six-year-old feel such debilitating shame?
>
> Almost immediately after asking myself the question, I began to remember my parents' words: 'Oh, look at the cry-baby!... Who do you think you are, anyway?... You think you're unhappy? What do you think I feel after all I've given you?... Look, Little Miss Know-It-all... Pretending to be sick will get you nowhere... Can't you do anything right?... Do I have to do everything myself?... Oh, it's you... What do you want now?' (Jane Middleton-Moz 1990, pp.18–19)

It's easy to see why a child constantly hearing those kinds of messages would start to feel toxic and debilitating shame!

Another example of just how strong these emotions can be is a personal experience of a holiday we were on a few years ago. An incident occurred where one of our children ended up in an uncontrollable rage, and about what we couldn't understand: there didn't seem to be anything that would warrant such an outburst. It was so bad that we spent a long time afterwards trying to calm him down.

Later on, when we discussed this with our therapist, it became clear that something had triggered him into another time zone – a previous event in his life that had impacted him so much that he was then stuck in that place. The tactics that we would normally use to reach him just didn't work on that occasion. Of course, he eventually did calm down but the memory of the intensity of that overwhelming emotion for him has stuck in my mind.

> We become like the proverbial man who had too much to drink and lost his keys in the alley but looked for them under the lamp post because the light was better. (Middleton-Moz 1990)

I love the above quote as it relates to how a traumatised child may sometimes react in a way that seems totally unrelated to current events:

we try to look for the answer in the present but something else is happening for them – they are looking elsewhere, to another time, probably.

Another analogy that I've come across recently from Dan Hughes' teachings is called the Shield of Shame (see Figure 13.3). This shows the reactions you may get from a child stuck in that place of shame and how they respond to others. When they feel that incredibly overwhelming feeling of shame they hold up the shield to protect themselves. They will lie about what they've done ('It wasn't me'), even when you're standing there watching them do it! Then blame someone else ('Well, she hit me first'), then minimise what they've done ('I didn't hit him that hard'), and then of course rage at themselves, at things and at other people.

Figure 13.3 Shield of shame.

SO HOW CAN WE HELP A CHILD STUCK IN TOXIC SHAME?

First, and above all else, your relationship with the child is key. Attunement, to begin with, and then the interactive repair must follow quickly to bring that relationship back into the right state. Think about PACE which we looked at in Part 2 and find ways to build your relationship with the child so that, when toxic shame is triggered, the strength of the relationship will make the child feel safe enough to let you into their pain.

Second, you need to be very mindful of the language you use with children who have experienced early trauma and how you communicate with them. They are hypersensitive to any new feelings of shame that will take them back to the toxic shame of the past. Your tone of voice, sarcasm or playful banter can sometimes be a trigger for these children. Stern looks, harsh raised voices, demanding eye contact, being ignored, discouragement – these can all add to the toxic shame they already feel.

Third, validate the child's feelings. As we looked at with PACE, accepting the child's inner world is vitally important in helping him to see that *he* is not bad. One way you can do this is to acknowledge when things are difficult for you too: 'I know it's hard to control your anger; I find it hard, too.' And 'Everyone feels frustrated sometimes.'

My son was in a 'Circle of Friends' group at school. In such a group, an adult facilitates a discussion with a group of children about friendship issues: how can you make friends, how do you know if someone doesn't want to be your friend, and so on. In this one instance, the facilitator was showing the children a picture of a scenario where two children were playing: one broke the other's toy by accident but the other one then grabbed his friend's toy and broke it in a rage. A normal scenario of course! However, the facilitator then said (with the very best of intentions), 'Of course, none of us would do that, would we?', to which my son hung his head in shame because he would do that and he knows it.

> *This kind of approach will only make a child feel that their inner world is so ugly and terrible that nobody else would do that – they are isolated and alone in their very powerful emotions.*

A better way to deal with this might be to say, 'We all feel like doing that, don't we…but what might happen if we did that?' (helping the children understand cause and effect) and 'What might be a better way to react?' (helping them to problem-solve and to come up with other ways of resolving a conflict).

Finally, teach the children how to contain their reactions. You will need to do this for them at first. Think about 'time in' and bring a troubled child close to you so that you can regulate his emotions – help him to breathe deeply and to relax. Give the children techniques to help calm themselves down. For example, use a self-selection card system: a set of cards showing various calming activities that a child can choose to do whenever he feels the need. Activities could include colouring, listening to music, stretching, sorting pencils and pens – whatever the child finds relaxing and is quick and easy to do. (This idea is taken from Louise Bomber's book, *Inside I'm Hurting*.)

Remember that, above all else, the repair of the relationship is the most important aspect.

Chapter 14

IDENTITY

Knowing who you are and where you come from is an important aspect in life. When you see TV programmes of celebrities trying to trace their family tree, you can see the impact it has on them. For myself, it's something that's fascinated me too as all my grandparents died either before I was born or very soon after. I had no relationship with them and it feels like there's a hole in my experience and in my understanding of my roots.

What makes up our identity? There are many different aspects, including our background, heritage, religion, culture, beliefs, likes, dislikes, race, gender – and physical attributes like hair colour and eyes. Many things come together to make us who we are and give us a sense of who we are – our sense of identity.

Our relationships are also important to how we see ourselves:

We see ourselves through the eyes of other people…even to the extent of incorporating their views of us into our own self-concept. (Cooley 1902)

What other people think about us is important to how we view ourselves – no more so than when we are growing up, and no person's view is more important than our parents'. You can understand, then, why a child who has not had the nurturing environment she needed would end up with a poor sense of identity. At the core of her being, she feels that he is unworthy and unlovable.

Also for children who are in the care system or adopted there is the very real fact that they don't have the information about their past. Like me with my grandparents: I can ask my parents, of course, but there will always be a few gaps for me. However, for children who have experienced immense trauma, the past is not something they necessarily want to think about – there just may be too many unanswered questions.

A child with a poor sense of identity might struggle with the following.

LIKES AND DISLIKES

The child may struggle to identify her likes and dislikes. If asked what she wants to drink, for example, she may find that a difficult question and may get annoyed and frustrated with having to come up with an answer. Hand in hand with this is the need to be liked by others, so she will go along with what others say and very often change her preferences to suit those around him. There is no strong sense of who she is and what he likes.

ROLE

The child may be uncertain about her role within the family, classroom or peer group. This gives her a feeling of not belonging and can isolate him even more than she is already.

PAIN

The child may show little response to pain, or even over-react to minor injury. We talked about this in the symptoms chapter in Part 1: blood can be running down her leg but she makes no sound – or a tiny pinprick in her finger and she brings the house down.

EYE CONTACT

The child may struggle with eye contact. This is linked to the child's strong feeling of worthlessness and when we look into her eyes, she feels very vulnerable.

SELF-REGULATION AND IMPULSE CONTROL

The child may struggle to regulate herself and control her impulses. This will be explored in more depth in the next chapter but, suffice to say, it is a sign of poor identity when a child finds it very difficult to regulate her emotions and demonstrates a lack of cause-and-effect thinking.

PEER RELATIONSHIPS

Peer relationships are a constant battle for vulnerable children. When a child has a strong sense of who she is, her character, his abilities and the knowledge that she is loved by others, she can then have healthy relationships with others. Children who don't have a strong sense of who they are will either be constantly trying to please, keeping away from others, or creating a false personality to convince others they are OK.

EMPATHY

A child with poor identity will also struggle with empathy. Again, this is a topic we will cover in more detail in the next chapter.

There are lots of ways we can help children develop their sense of a good, positive, strong identity.

One of those ways is to encourage them to make choices by picking a win-win scenario. For example, instead of saying, 'What would you like to drink?' (too much choice), you could say, 'Would you like blackcurrant or orange?' Either one is fine with you so it gives them a chance to choose. However, this may still be too much choice for them to start with, so you may just need to say, 'I think orange today as I know you love orange.' This takes away their need to choose and also instils in them the fact that you notice what they like, which will help them to notice it too.

I've found that, with my own children, giving them too much choice creates anxiety and then I get stressed as they spend ages figuring out what they want: taking the sweets, then putting them back, then taking them again. Make it an easier decision but with some choice on their part if you can.

You can also play games around their likes and dislikes. For example, you could show them lots of photos of things and places and get them to say, 'like', 'don't like'. This works well with a group of children as they can then see that everyone feels differently. We did a similar game recently during therapy which involved me acting out something that happened on our holiday and then my child saying whether that was something he loved or hated. This gave us the opportunity to talk about the hate stuff without having to say, 'What didn't you like about the holiday then?' Less confrontational, more playful – and it gave him a chance to say what he liked and didn't like.

One of the tasks in our education curriculum that often comes up and which can be a very difficult one for the vulnerable children we are concerned with is the family tree or 'growing up' projects, such as 'Bring in your baby photos' or 'Who do you resemble in your family?' They may not know or be able to respond to these things and, worse, the discussions may also bring painful memories and triggers to their mind and emotions. However, what we can do to help a child who struggles with this is to talk about siblings if they are together with them: 'You have the same smile as your brother' or 'You and your sister have the same shaped eyes.' This helps the child to understand who he is. You can also give him a mirror to help him look at and talk about his own features. What does he like about his face? How can he show someone else he is sad? These simple methods help them to become more aware in a positive way of who they are and how they are seen by others.

There are many resources around these days that help promote difference and diversity. There's one children's book, for example, called *Picnic in the Park* by Joe Griffiths and Tony Pilgrim (2007). This book is a simple picture story book that talks about a picnic where lots of different people come: there are tall children, mixed-race families, foster children, same-sex couples, single people – a whole range of different people from different lifestyles and backgrounds. There is also a section in the back of the book where the child is encouraged to put a photo of his own family into the picnic in the park. This is a great book to help children come to terms with identity.

Another way to help children with identity is to offer them a wide range of sensory experiences to help them develop and talk about the associated feelings. There are many interactive museums around that allow this kind of experience. Make sure, though, that you contain them as much as possible in these environments – sensory less! On a school trip, therefore, you may wish to keep numbers low – for example, take a group of children aside to help them deal with any issues that arise from the sensory experiences created by the environment around them.

Be careful not to overload on positivity for vulnerable children: when they are unsure of who they are and what they like or dislike, the experience of adults being overly gushy about how brilliant they are at something can sometimes have an opposing effect – that is, the child *not* wanting to try in case he fails and disappoints you. The child concerned will very often sabotage nice experiences as she feels she doesn't deserve them. If you know she is good at sport, for example, and encourage her to take part, don't be surprised if she gives up very quickly – or sabotages the experience in some other way. After all, not trying is better than trying and failing as far as she is concerned.

Try to label emotions and feelings for them when you are going through experiences together, so that they can learn to identify them themselves in time. This feels very strange to begin with but you have to imagine these children are much younger than their chronological age. You may normally say to a two-year-old, 'Wow, look at how your hands look in the sunlight!' or 'Can you feel the sea and sand in between your toes? It feels all squishy and cold.' These kinds of interactions would appear normal with a smaller child but vulnerable children need to be taught how to notice things about themselves and others – even if they are 11 years old.

Finally, children who are adopted or in the care system will constantly be trying to make sense of their story, and their past – in a formal way or otherwise. Communicate with their parents and carers as much as you can to make sure you are all aware of areas that may be difficult for a particular child at any given time. It helps a child to know that everyone who is involved with her is working together to help her.

Chapter 15

EMPATHY

From birth, when babies' fingers instinctively cling to those of adults, their bodies and brains seek an intimate connection – a bond made possible by empathy, the remarkable ability to love and to share the feelings of others. (Perry and Szalavitz 2010)

Empathy is something that starts to develop in those early years through our experiences with others. The mirror neurons we discussed earlier help us to see how others feel and to mirror that, which leads us to understand that others feel differently too. We can start to see things from another's point of view. This is something that I had always believed you either had or didn't have, but I am beginning to see that our early experiences shape our capacity to show empathy.

Here are the stages of empathy development and what you should typically see at these ages:

- 0–2 years:

    ○ By soothing an infant, you'll help him learn to comfort himself and, eventually, to comfort others.

    ○ Toddlers are sensitive to the feelings of their friends and will often mimic their emotions – a necessary precursor to empathy.

    ○ Empathy needs to be repeatedly modelled and encouraged in toddlers before it becomes a part of their behaviour.

- 3–4 years:

    ○ Threes can make the connection between emotions and desires, and they can respond to a friend's distress with simple soothing gestures.

- ○ Sometimes pre-schoolers can only relate to the feelings of others if they share the same feelings and perspective on a situation.

- ○ Fours are capable of seeing a situation from another person's perspective. Yet they need to know that not all reactions to feelings are OK.

- 5–6 years:

- ○ With their ever-increasing vocabulary, fives and sixes love to share their feelings, and discussions about emotions will help them develop a better understanding of the feelings of others.

- ○ Fives and sixes are learning how to read others' feelings through their actions, gestures, and facial expressions – an essential empathy and social skill.

- ○ Through an adult's modelling of, and encouraging, empathy, nursery children and early years will learn how to become compassionate members of a caring community.

(Poole, Miller and Booth Church 2005)

For children who have had a difficult start in life, a lack of empathy is very typical. This manifests itself in lots of different ways: indiscriminate affection, lack of eye contact, weak cause-and-effect thinking or give-and-take mentality, cruelty to others, destructiveness, unhealthy interest in violence and death, unhealthy peer relationships and poorly developed conscience.

All of these difficult areas actually intertwine and overlap so that many of the strategies will be the same. For example, building a child's sense of self will also help him develop empathy: the more a child knows who he is, the more he can distinguish between himself and others and see the distinctive differences.

You will need to explicitly model many of the things you are trying to teach your most vulnerable children, as we know that they see and hear everything we do!

So, model empathy in your relationships and make it overt: when you're talking about a friend who's struggling, you could say words to the effect of 'Oh dear, Sally is having a really difficult time. Maybe we could take her some flowers.' You can also create opportunities to show empathy: involve the child in sending a get well card to another teacher, make up a charity food box at Christmas, participate in a sponsored something for charity and talk about the people it will be helping. School is a great place for this as you tend to want to do things as a class to help others. Find projects that will help them to understand how different people live and how we can help in some way.

Use the PACE approach with vulnerable children as much as you can. Empathic listening is about accepting their inner world and allowing them to explore their feelings. Try to listen in a way that will model to them how to listen to others and encourage them to do the same.

You may need to help the vulnerable child to know when he is in pain. For example, my daughter fell over at a friend's house. It was quite a bad fall, blood down her leg, no need for stitches or a hospital but, nonetheless, I expected a cry or at least a whimper – but nothing! She came and found me and just said, 'I fell over.' I looked at her knee and said straight away, 'Oh dear, that looks painful. It's really bad. Sit down and let me get something to wipe it. Are you OK?' I made a big fuss of her to try to get her to see that, actually, that should be painful – it's OK to be in pain.

Such a reaction is hard to affect sometimes as our tendency is to try and tell them it's OK, nothing to worry about, stop crying, you're too big a girl to be crying. But such vulnerable children as the ones we're concerned with need to know that it's OK and, in fact, appropriate, to cry when you're in pain and to need comfort from someone – and not to have to cope with it on your own.

I would encourage you to read Dr Bruce Perry's book on this subject called *Born for Love* (Perry and Szalavitz 2010). It's an excellent book that goes into great detail about empathy and why it is so important to us all.

Chapter 16

TRUST

Trust is a difficult area for adopted and looked-after children and children with attachment difficulties. Why should they trust adults? Some have not been a great example to them so far, whether they've experienced a neglectful, abusive or inconsistent start in life – and they may have then been moved around adults like hand-me-down clothes. This may seem a harsh thing to say but sometimes their realities are harsh!

Why is trust such a big problem for these children? The online dictionary by Farlex gives us many definitions of trust but these three were particularly relevant I thought:

- reliance on the integrity, strength, ability, surety of a person or thing

- confident expectation of something; hope

- a person on whom, or thing on which, one relies.

All three of these areas have broken down for many vulnerable children.

For the child with an emotionally or physically absent parent, being able to rely on that parent was futile. For the child who has had a parent promise that it will never happen again, confident expectation or hope is non-existent – and the child in an abusive situation in whatever way has not been kept safe, with no-one to rely on.

All three areas of trust broken! No wonder they find trusting other adults difficult.

Why is trust such an important and fundamental concept for us to acquire? What we experience repeatedly becomes the norm for us. It becomes what we expect to see and happen in all circumstances. Repetition is so important – the more times a baby's needs are met consistently, the more the baby can trust.

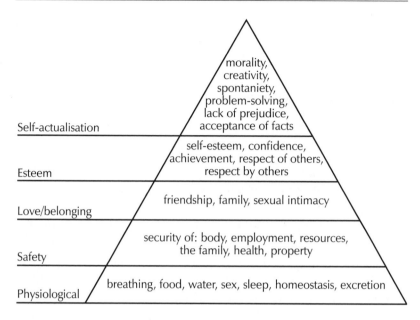

Figure 16.1 Maslow's hierarchy of needs.

Maslow's hierarchy of needs was created and published in 1943 by Abraham Maslow. He subsequently wrote a paper on *A Theory of Human Motivation*, where he proposed that all human beings must have their basic needs met before they can move onto experience and accept a higher level of need being met.

Figure 16.1 shows Maslow's pyramid with the bottom layers of physiological needs such as food, water and sleep being the most essential. Until those needs are met we can't move onto feeling safe and secure and then a sense of belonging and love, then to feel self-esteem and finally be able to be creative and find meaning and purpose in life.

The problems arise when our needs are not met at those lower levels. The vulnerable children we've been talking about will be more concerned about where the next meal is coming from than how to do their times tables. Coming back to the reptilian part of the brain, survival becomes the driving force for them.

Learning is not a priority – survival is.

It may sound very dramatic but it is the unconscious, primal emotions that drive these children and keep them in a state of anxiety.

Another reason why trust is important is to do with becoming independent. I often hear teachers talk about needing to move our kids towards independence, for example, 'They are too old to have me write messages home – they should remember.' Or 'They need to take some responsibility now they are 11 years old.'

The problem with this is that you cannot be truly independent if you've not been truly dependent *on someone.*

As we can see from the aforementioned definition of trust, children who have experienced early trauma have probably not had many people to depend on.

The most important reason why trust is essential for these children is, I believe, to break the cycle they are in. Until they can experience trusting relationships and really connect with people, they are at risk of growing up as dysfunctional adults and, in turn, having children that they then cannot parent – or teach to trust.

How does this then impact you as someone trying to teach them or help them? How do you deal with the trust dilemma?

It is difficult to get children to let go and trust you, especially when they will not have much time with you each day. They may also appear to trust but, in reality, they are holding back to see what might happen: Will you let them down? Will you do what you say? Will you hurt them in some way?

Of course none of us trust people completely until we get to know them and, in any case, we demonstrate different degrees of trust with different people. However, not being able to trust has a more damaging effect on the vulnerable children we are concerned with: it stops them from being able to be at ease with people; it makes learning hard work because they are constantly worried about what may happen. Their minds and feelings are clogged up with anxiety that makes it doubly difficult to be open to learn and experience new things.

To illustrate just how long it takes them to learn to trust, here's a story about one of my sons. Just for some context, he was seven years old and had been with us for three years.

Every time he had a bath, we got to the point where he had his hair rinsed. I used a bowl and mixed the water from the taps in the sink and then poured it over his head. Every time, for three years, he'd asked to feel the water before I poured it on his head. This was always a reminder to me that he really didn't trust that I would do the best for him!

Then, one day, he said he wasn't going to test the water. I nearly fell off my seat. Wow, I thought, we are making progress; so, on that day, he didn't put his hand in the bowl – he just let me pour the water on his head. It was a defining moment for me.

Of course, you may be thinking, great – now I bet he trusts you completely? Well, it's not that simple, I guess – he went straight back to asking to test the water the next time he had a bath and has continued ever since.

Building trust is not something that happens overnight – it takes time, patience and the understanding that the smallest glimpse of hope is enough to build on and help that child to learn to trust other adults as well.

WHAT THEN CAN YOU DO TO HELP THAT CHILD TO BUILD TRUST?

First, allocate the child a key adult. This adult needs to be someone who, as much as you know, can be a constant, reliable and available person who he can go to when things are difficult – someone who works at building trust with him and is on his side. This can help him with changes of routine at school, club or in the learning environment. The adult can also learn about the child, understand his needs and anxieties and try to mediate with others involved.

Second, the way you relate to the child is very important. Make sure you keep to the things you say as much as possible. He will remember everything even if he doesn't seem to be listening. Don't make promises you can't keep. Understand that he is watching your every move: what you model for him can make a huge difference to his development.

Finally, know that it is not personal. Any way the child reacts to you is not necessarily because of you. The closer he feels to you, the more he may take out his anger, loss and grief on you. Stay strong for him in these circumstances especially, and know that any small trust he feels for adults is a step in the right direction.

Chapter 17

CONTROL AND SELF-RELIANCE

Control is to 'exercise authoritative or dominating influence over', and to dominate means to 'have control or power over another. To exercise such control or power' (online dictionary by Farlex).

From all that you've read so far about children who have experienced early trauma, you know that much of their lives have been about other people being in control of them – their birth parents, social services, foster carers, doctors, therapists, adoptive parents, the courts – all deciding what happens to them and helping or hindering their development in one way or another.

As Bowlby explains in his early work on attachment, if a child does not have a safe base to come back to, he finds exploring and participating in the world around him difficult. When you consider the types of environment some children have been exposed to – domestic violence, chaotic family life, poverty, deprivation, abuse – where they were completely powerless to do anything about it, you can understand why they would want to control the environment they are in now. To be out of control is very scary and unpredictable.

You will probably recognise when a child is trying to control his surroundings, but sometimes it can be very subtle and covert. One of our therapists said to me once that she had just realised my son was actually controlling everything in the session: the tasks we did, who did what, who sat where. She would start out feeling in control of the session and where it might go and then end up thinking, 'How did that happen? We ended up doing everything he wanted.' I know the reason he felt he had to do that was because he was feeling unsafe and anxious. He doesn't know, of course, that he's trying to control things – these are primitive, instinctive reactions children express as a result of the attachment difficulties they have.

Control can be very overt in terms of the vulnerable child saying and demanding you do what he wants – but it can also be *covert* in terms of his charming, manipulative way of moving you to do what he wants. The important point to understand here is the *reason* he is doing it: he is not trying to manipulate in a malicious way – the attempt to control his environment is coming from a place of fear.

WHAT ARE THE SIGNS TO LOOK OUT FOR IN A CHILD WHO IS ATTEMPTING TO CONTROL HIS ENVIRONMENT?

Confrontation

Some children try to control in a very upfront, confrontational way – arguing, being defiant, shouting, screaming – basically, you do it their way or no way at all.

Physically running away

There's no better way to control something than run away from it. How can you make them do something they don't want to do if you can't catch them?

Dissociation

We talked about this earlier – that 'tuning out' state that some children get into when things are just too much and the body or mind shuts down in some way. They become overwhelmed with the need to control and zone out of their environment instead of running away or being confrontational.

Taking charge of others

You will probably see this more in the case of older siblings who may have looked after their younger siblings. They find it incredibly difficult to release the grip of control on others and to let adults take charge, especially as that would mean trusting the adult to meet their needs and that of their siblings.

Remember that any controlling behaviour is the result of underlying panic, pain and fear.

I have included self-reliance in this section, as it tends to coincide with the need to control. If a child has had to look after himself and other siblings, he has had to become self-reliant. He doesn't trust others to meet his needs so he will get his needs met in whichever way possible – controlling environments and people to make that happen.

This can be seen in very subtle ways: the child struggling to open a bottle but unwilling to ask for help, the child who is unable to do his work at school but is frightened of asking for help, or, in a more extreme case, the child who will go out of his way to get what he needs from others – whether by lying, stealing or manipulating his way into others' affections – for the purposes of getting something he feels he needs.

Vulnerable children can also be very primal in their survival instinct – making sure they are the one that everyone likes. This surprised me when our three arrived. They had been together virtually from birth so I assumed they would be a tight unit, which they are at times: if they think one of their number will be hurt, the other two rally round. However, if one is in trouble, the others make it very clear that they didn't do it; they will say, 'Mum, I'm being good!'

At the end of the day, that basic need to survive and be loved is very powerful.

As I mentioned earlier, self-reliance is different from independence. What people see from our children in the way they are outgoing at times, they mistake for independence and confidence; it's actually self-reliance which, at its root, says, 'I don't need anyone else; you will not tell me what to do; I don't believe what you say and I will make sure I get my needs met without you.' This can be very hard as a parent but also as a professional trying to help them learn and develop – the constant questioning of what you say and disregard for your advice and knowledge is hard to take. But, again, remember that it is not personal. They don't trust most people and it takes time to build that trust.

HOW THEN DO WE HELP THEM WITH THEIR CONTROL AND SELF-RELIANCE?

First, strike the balance between nurture and structure. Remember the metal box with a velvet lining: a good, strong structure lined with compassion, always being aware of the impact of trauma on the child.

It's important to be there for them when you say you will and do what you say you will do. Actions speak louder than words we are told. Well, it's true and definitely so in the case of vulnerable children. They need to see, hear and feel that what you say is believable. This is a hard one, I know, as circumstances change, but the more you can do it – or at least help them through it if you can't keep the promise – the better.

Try to give age-appropriate responsibility. If you have a child who has experienced early trauma in a school environment or a club and you think, 'John would be a great mentor for so and so', or 'I think Mary is ready to be a helper in this area', just remember all you know of them from what you've read so far. A child may fluctuate between behaving like their peers and then regressing to a much younger emotional age. I have this at times with my youngest, who is progressing brilliantly and often seems very much his chronological age. However, he was asked to mentor another boy at school at one point, which I did feel he might not be ready for, but I let it happen. After a few weeks the teacher came and said they'd had to stop the mentoring as my lad wasn't responding well to the responsibility – that was because he was not yet where he needed to be in terms of his own development.

Help them take some control in making choices – as with developing identity. Make sure they are win-win choices. However, be aware that a child may seem like he wants to take control but then can't deal with the responsibility of that control, so may very well sabotage it. For example, I know a child who loves to say what film the rest of the family *must* watch but then, when it's put on, he often doesn't want to watch it and makes it difficult for the others to watch too.

When thinking about consequences and what behaviour to challenge pick your battles carefully. Some things are not important enough. I heard of a mother once who was having problems with her son getting dressed for school: he insisted on wearing coloured socks and she knew the uniform code stipulated black socks. It became such a battle every morning that, eventually, she had to speak to the school and say that he would be wearing coloured socks. Some issues are just not worth battling over for the time being. In time, however, the child may feel secure enough to relinquish that area of control, but until then, let it go.

Chapter 18

SELF-REGULATION

WHAT IS SELF-REGULATION AND HOW DOES IT DEVELOP?

Self-regulation is the ability to control your urges and impulses, change your behaviour if needed and follow other people's instructions – like your mum and dad or the teacher.

It is also about being able to soothe yourself when you are hurt emotionally – to know that it is not the end of the world if you miss out on a sweet this time. Life will be good to you again.

From around 12 months old, babies start to develop the ability to control their urges and can listen to others and do what they are told. Notice I said 'can' – that doesn't mean they will.

As the child grows, so does his ability to stop himself from doing something he wants to do but is told not to – like hitting his sibling. Also, he starts to do things that he is asked to do even though he doesn't want to do it – like tidy his room.

Without the ability to self-regulate, children will grow into adults who find it very hard to function and learn, or to build and hold down relationships – to manage life in general.

In securely attached children the development stages are typically as follows.

Self-regulation begins between 12 and 18 months. They are more aware of social expectations and develop an ability to change behaviour when asked by an adult. This stage does, of course, require an adult to be there, helping and guiding.

By 24 months, children start to develop self-control and the ability to follow instructions even when the adult is not present.

By 36 months, most children can internalise adults' instructions and wishes. They will act and behave according to what they believe adults expect. Their self-regulation now needs less guidance from adults.

Interestingly, self-regulation is linked to brain development and bodily responses to stress in particular. Your brain and body are constantly sensing and responding to the needs you have. Specialised sensors monitor internal and external environments. When they sense a need or a problem – you are hungry or stressed, for example – they activate your brain's alarm systems in order to act on that need.

We are concerned here with children who have not had the help and guidance in their early years to learn to self-regulate. When they feel stress from internal or external factors, they are at risk in a number of areas – persistent tantrums and aggression, impulsive behaviours or difficulty regulating sleep and diet, to name but a few.

What helps the stress response to develop adequately is repetitive exposure to needs being met in a controllable way.

So, for example, a child will know that, when they're hungry and crying, they will have food and be satisfied. They learn what the feeling of being hungry is for a start, and then that the need can be met. As they grow, they know how that need is met and can regulate that on their own – asking for food, for example, or getting it for themselves as they become more independent. They can also say when they are full and when to stop eating.

However, for children who have not had such a consistent response, they will be confused about conflicting feelings around hunger, for example. Some children who have not been fed regularly will find food a real issue. They may not be able to tell when they are hungry and when they are full – and they will definitely have anxiety around the availability of food.

A big issue for such children is around understanding their emotions and the internal alarm responses. A fearful child may be sullen and angry, unaware that they are actually anxious about a change of routine in the classroom. A hungry child may be distracted, irritable and uncooperative, unaware that what they really feel is hunger. This is sometimes hard enough to discern in ourselves as adults: at times you may not identify that you are anxious about something, when you can't sleep or your appetite changes.

The point here is that children who have experienced early trauma will have more difficulty than most in identifying their feelings and the things that cause them stress. Those around them very often misunderstand them.

HOW CAN YOU IDENTIFY POOR SELF-REGULATION?

Children with under-developed self-regulation will present with many different signs.

Some are:

- impulsive behaviour

- hypersensitivity to transitions and change

- over-reaction to minor challenges

- inattentiveness

- physical hyperactivity

- frequent tantrums at later stages of development

- inability to know when they are hungry or thirsty – they may ask for food or drink constantly.

Once you identify those for whom self-regulation is poor, there are some ways you can help them to learn how to regulate themselves.

Model self-control and self-regulation through your words and actions. For example, you might say something like, 'I have had a difficult day and need to take some time out to feel better, so I'm going to sit here for a moment.'

Provide structure where possible. The more vulnerable children need strong boundaries and structures since they will not have the internal guide to help them – as I've said a few times in this book. Recall the guiding principle around structure in terms of helping children to regulate: if you leave them to have 'free play', they tend to get themselves wound up and dysregulated – and then it takes a lot of effort to help them calm down again.

Ensure predictability whenever possible. The children need to know when things will happen and that they actually will happen. For example, knowing when snack breaks, lunch time and home time is can be all-important to them. If they know what's coming, they can relax a little and concentrate on the task in front of them. Of course, they may need to be reminded occasionally, as their anxiety levels can be very high.

Anticipate transitions and change wherever possible. Write things down for the parents as the children may not take in and pass on verbal instructions. Make sure you communicate as much as possible with the parents or carers so that they can reassure the child as well. It is also helpful if you know the types of strategies and techniques the parents are using with their child so that you can do the same.

Identify those who are most impulsive and poorly self-regulated and try to keep them apart. They will probably gravitate towards each other, but that will only make things harder to manage in your environment.

Remember that *children with poor self-regulation are very often comfortable with chaos* and may try to create an atmosphere of chaos – counter this with structure and boundaries.

Remember that *self-regulation takes time for all children* – it does not develop overnight but it is such an essential part of being a functioning adult and well worth the time and energy it takes for you to understand and know how to help them.

Chapter 19

CAUSE-AND-EFFECT THINKING

Cause-and-effect thinking is about understanding the connection between an action and a consequence – that everything we do has an impact on something or someone. It's about having the capability to think through our actions (What might happen if I do this?) and then making a decision based on all the different scenarios that might occur.

This process develops very early in childhood when a child learns that they can influence the environment around them. They can make people smile and laugh; they can get the attention of others by screaming; there is a reaction from others to what they do or don't do.

This realisation that they can impact the world around them starts at around eight months of age. A child does simple things that make something else happen – they begin to notice the relationship between events and the effect others have on their world too.

One example of this is when a baby bangs something on a table: they notice the noise it makes and the reaction they get, and then do it again, and again and again!

By the age of 18 months, the child begins to experiment with the outcomes of things. What happens if I use a different object? How will that change the sound?

At around 36 months of age, children show they are beginning to understand the correlation between cause and effect – they seem to make predictions about what might happen and even reflect on what caused it to happen (California Department of Education [CDE] 2005).

An example of this final stage is when you are watching a film with a child and they start to say what they think might happen next. This shows they are processing cause-and-effect thinking – the outcome of actions taken.

However, for children who have experienced early trauma, it's a very different story. If you consider how limited their environment is likely to have been in terms of stimulation and interaction, their development will have consequently been severely impaired. They will not have had the same experience of games and toys that help them develop cause-and-effect thinking, such as pop-up toys: push the red button and the rabbit pops up; pull the lever and a noise comes out.

Children with Attachment Difficulties will not necessarily make the connections between their behaviour and what follows. For example they might have hit their sister, thrown lots of things around in their room and then asked for some ice-cream. They do not understand our frustrations at this kind of behaviour, which seems to say that they don't care what they do, when in fact they just have not made the link between their 'bad' behaviour and the 'reward' that follows. This is one of the reasons why traditional parenting techniques are difficult for children with attachment difficulties to respond to because they assume a child can make those connections.

If you recall the section on brain development – and especially the neurons and synapses that go through the pruning process – it is plain to see that, if a child does not develop cause-and-effect thinking, if he is not getting the stimuli that demonstrate the outcome of actions and the reciprocity of relationships, then that connection in the brain will fall away. In other words, parts of the brain that are needed in order to follow the process of cause and effect are not wired properly. This means that, for a child who seems to have no understanding of consequences, it's not necessarily that they don't care about what might happen if they hit someone else, they just hadn't thought about it – that part of the process isn't there.

The problem when trying to help a child who has difficulty with cause-and-effect thinking is that punishment and consequences won't fix things for him. He will probably not understand the connection between what he has done – the action – and the consequence. It doesn't mean anything to him. Remember also the toxic shame he may feel: punishment tends to induce more shame and leave the child trapped in his unworthy feelings.

THINGS YOU MIGHT SEE IN A CHILD WITH DIFFICULTY PROCESSING CAUSE AND EFFECT

Poor impulse control

The child will think something and then do it. Whereas most people have a process in the middle which is about thinking through the consequences of what they might want to do, that part is missing in the minds of some children: they will have the impulse to do something and then just do it.

Indiscriminate affection

As already stated, this is a very typical symptom of a child with attachment difficulties and, again, it shows a lack of thought regarding the outcome: Who might this person be? How safe is he or she? There's no 'stranger danger' awareness for such children so they need to be watched very carefully in environments involving strangers – they can get themselves into dangerous situations without knowing it.

Inability to share and give

Understanding that 'if I give this toy to someone I will get it back at some point' can be a difficulty. Again, this links to empathy and knowing that you can share with others.

Poorly developed conscience

It may seem, at times, that the child doesn't know the difference between right and wrong and, of course, he may not. This is not just because he doesn't think through the consequences of his actions but also because he hasn't had the role models and boundaries that teach him right from wrong. He may have been in many different homes with many different rules and expectations. Knowing that it's not OK to swear at someone else, for example, doesn't come naturally to a child who has been sworn at constantly.

Extreme control issues and destructiveness

Why would the child want to relinquish control of a situation when he doesn't understand that others do actually have his best interests at heart? As mentioned in the control chapter, the child has had little control of his life, so he would be very reluctant to hand that over right now. When you see a child destroying possessions, it's probably to do with his lack of cause-and-effect thinking, as well as the belief that he doesn't deserve to have nice things. This is an area that I hear many adopters talk about – children who destroy their bedrooms time and again with no apparent regard for the value of things.

Cruelty to others – whether animals or humans

This again shows a lack of thought or concern for the outcomes of their actions.

Lying and stealing

This, again, is about poor impulse control – using external stimuli to soothe inner hurt and fear of what might happen. The consequences and punishment for being 'bad' in the past may have been incredibly severe. Why would a child then want to own up to doing something he considers to be bad? What might happen as a result?

Lack of concrete thought

The concrete thought process, according to the medical dictionary, is:

> A stage in the development of the cognitive thought processes in the child. During this phase, thought becomes increasingly logical and coherent so that the child is able to classify, sort, order, and organize facts while still being incapable of generalizing or dealing in abstractions. Problem-solving is accomplished in a concrete, systematic fashion based on what is perceived, keeping to the literal meaning of words, as in applying the word horse to a particular animal and not to horses in general. In Piaget's classification, this stage occurs between 7 and 11 years of age, is preceded by syncretic thinking, and is followed by abstract thinking. (online dictionary by Farlex)

For many of these vulnerable children, logical and coherent thought and being able to express those thoughts is rare. In the case of our own children, it is sometimes very difficult to understand what they are saying or for them to order the thoughts and words in their minds to make an articulate statement.

Faced with impaired brain development and faulty wiring, we can start to think it's a hopeless task trying to help such children but *that is not the case*. Connections can still be made and repaired. They may never function as fully as they might have done, but with proper help and understanding, these children will be able to reach a stage where all these difficulties become something they can manage and adapt to.

SO WHAT CAN YOU DO TO HELP?

Find ways to help the child think through scenarios – not in the heat of the moment or when they are in a state of stress about making a decision but when they are calm. For example, thinking maps, or mind maps as they used to be called, are a great way to help children arrange their thoughts. They help children to access all parts of the brain so that they can be as creative as possible. Sit a child down and think about a situation he may have been in – an argument with a friend, for example. What are the possible actions he could have taken and what are the possible outcomes to those actions?

Another way to help a child to think through outcomes is on-the-spot thinking. One of my own children loves to climb trees – I think he may be a monkey in his parallel universe. Anyway, when he wants to attempt a particularly dangerous climb that I don't want him to do, he comes to me and says, 'Mum, can I climb that tree?' 'Well,' I say, 'what might happen if you climb that tree?' 'I might fall,' he says. 'Yes', I reply. 'Or I might get stuck,' he says. 'Yes,' I reply. 'If I climb, then my friend might want to climb too and he's too little to get up that tree,' he says. And I respond with, 'Yes, so what might happen to him then?' And on we go. You get the picture: he is doing the thinking and I don't need to tell him it's not a great idea, as he will eventually say, 'OK, maybe not today.'

Do activities and games that involve cause and effect. We tend to think older children won't want to play with baby toys but I've noticed that if you put any children – vulnerable or not – in a room of soft toys, ball pits, noisy toys, etc., they all play with them. They don't have to be toys designed for babies or toddlers but they can be. Many games and activities centre around cause and effect.

Make sure you create lots of opportunities for sensory and exploratory play as this helps children to experience the development stages they have missed.

As I watch adults with children, I notice that we don't often respond quickly to them. We are conditioned to believe that they should come lower down in the pecking order to adults. For example, a child runs up to you and you're in a conversation with someone. They blurt out something and your immediate reaction is, 'The adults are talking here – don't interrupt.' I understand why we do this and I've done it myself many times – until recently, when I heard a psychologist talk on this subject particularly for children who have experienced trauma.

What he said was that the child needs to know that they are important to you. They have not felt or been important to others in the past and this compounds their sense of shame, which we know is not a good place for them to be. Of course you need to have conversations with adults and get on with other things, but there is a way to respond quickly to the child's need without making them feel unimportant.

In the example of being in a conversation with another adult when a child interrupts, what you can do is pause the conversation and say, 'Are you OK, Billy? Do you need something right now?' Very often, he won't, but he just wants to know you will respond. The other adult should be secure enough to accept this – and, of course, if you can explain to the adult beforehand that this might happen, all the better. That one moment of attention given to the child will very often appease him and he'll go off to play. However, what we tend to do is exacerbate his anxiety by brushing him off when we could just take that moment to make him feel special and that we see him. This helps develop his understanding that he does have an impact in the world: when he speaks, people listen!

Chapter 20

MEMORY AND ORGANISATION

Memories are peculiar. They can be very clear and accurate at times, then at other times very blurred, confusing and who knows whether they are factual or not? Memory is the ability to be able to hold a thought in mind and carry it forward to the future – remembering something that happened, for example, and recalling that in your mind at any given time.

Organisation, on the other hand, is about being able to bring together disparate parts to make a whole – bringing all the thoughts and ideas together to make something happen.

Dr Bruce Perry, in his field of work, talks about memory templates (Perry 2006, p.85). When we experience things repeatedly it creates a template in our brain – a blueprint, if you like, of that experience. For example, when you learn to drive a car, that ability is laid down in your brain: how to start the car, how to use the brakes, look in the mirrors, indicate, turn the steering wheel – all at the same time. Through repetition that ability is laid down as a blueprint in your brain.

What then happens is that we don't bother to think through all those sequences any more as the memory is set to repeat those actions. When we drive, we very rarely consciously think about the gears, the mirror or the brakes. It's only when something unusual happens, like a car pulls out in front, for example, or the lights change unexpectedly, that our minds kick into gear and we pay attention.

For children, these templates are being created daily, if not hourly. As they experience the same things over and over again, they develop blueprints that help form their memories.

For children who haven't had good patterns of interaction, the kind of templates they have are different to most other children.

They may not know, for example, what a good birthday is supposed to be like, or the appropriate way to behave with other children. They may not have had the formative experiences that most children will have had daily, so those 'blueprint' templates are not laid down for them.

The brains of these children are so focused on survival and they are so consumed with fear that being able to concentrate is incredibly difficult. They won't necessarily have heard or taken in that they need to be in school at 8:45 tomorrow for swimming, or that they need to ask their parents to come to an assembly next Tuesday. It's not that they can't remember later on; they just never actually heard or processed it in the first place. This, therefore, hinders the laying down of new memories. You may feel you are giving them consistent experiences but they are not concentrating enough to take in those experiences.

However, there is hope – new memories and templates can be created through repetitive, patterned experiences and interactions with others.

HOW CAN YOU TELL IF A CHILD HAS POOR MEMORY OR ORGANISATIONAL SKILLS?

The child will frequently forget what he is supposed to be doing. He may start a task and then not finish it as he has forgotten what to do. You ask him to go and get something and, by the time he gets there, he forgets what it was you asked for.

He is very often untidy with his possessions and clothing, showing little regard for cleanliness. This can be an issue with any child but, along with other symptoms, it can be an indicator that a child cannot organise themselves or their things enough to make things tidy. In addition, his handwriting may appear very sloppy and untidy, showing little care and attention to detail. This can be for a number of reasons, one being he cannot organise the letters, or he may have difficulty with fine motor skills.

He will regularly lose items or equipment or constantly forget to bring them in to school. He may know that Monday is swimming day but forget to bring his things in, or he may frequently forget to bring books or homework back to school. Of course, you may not be aware of this, as his parents might be very organised in helping him remember what he needs and often do things for him.

One of the frustrating aspects to this area of difficulty is that the children appear not to care about things. They may appear to be lazy or have a 'couldn't care less' attitude. They may seem to be deliberately forgetful, remembering sometimes but not at other times. This is usually not the case, however: a child may just be in a different place that day – something may have happened to trigger her forgetfulness, she may not have heard the instruction or she may not have understood but didn't want to tell anyone.

SOME OF THE WAYS YOU CAN HELP CHILDREN WITH THEIR MEMORY AND ORGANISATION SKILLS

- Play memory games with them to encourage their memory in a non-stressful environment – games like Pelmanism, where you have to find pairs of cards that match, or Kim's Game: have a tray of objects which the child looks at for a few minutes, then cover them up and ask the child to write down as many objects as he can remember.

- For some time they will need help to remember things, so lists and visual aids are helpful: a list of what needs to be in the child's school bag, for example. If possible, make sure school and home are using the same techniques as that reinforces the process for the child.

- Make sure that you divide long tasks and assignments into short bite-sized chunks so that the child can do each part in sequence and feel he has accomplished something.

- The relationship with the child is key to resolving most issues for children who have experienced early trauma. Make sure you continue to use PACE as you communicate with the child about things she has forgotten; try not to induce shame. Above all, be consistent and positive, remembering you are helping them to lay down those new memory templates that will help them function better in the future as they learn how to organise themselves.

Chapter 21

CHANGES AND TRANSITIONS

The dictionary has some interesting definitions of change:

- 'to move from one thing to another'

- 'to become different to'

- 'to lay aside, abandon or leave for another'

- 'to give and receive reciprocally, interchange' (online dictionary by Farlex).

A transition in sporting terms means:

- 'to change from defence to offence or offence to defence' (online dictionary by Farlex).

That's very apt when considering children who have experienced early trauma as it can very often feel like moving from a position of defence to offense and that switch can take place several times in a day!

Being able to know that change is OK can only come when you have a secure basis to place that on. For example, you know that if your mum goes away for an hour or so, she will come back. Children who live in a chaotic family environment do not have the stability and security to handle change very well. They have experienced so much change in their short lives – much of it not very good – that any hint of change from what they are used to in that moment can create unnecessary fear and anxiety.

We are all comfortable with what we know – whether it is a good or bad experience.

As humans, we seem to crave the known and fear the unknown. Why else is it called 'being out of your comfort zone' if you're not comfortable in it? For the children who have known little else in their lives, but seem 'content' with it, one may ask, 'How could they want that kind of chaos?' A fair question, but when that is all you've known, then the alternative of being in a calm, loving and safe environment can seem just as scary, if not more so. As a consequence, children from unsafe environments will often sabotage special events, treats, parties (the kind of things we expect children to love) but for most vulnerable children, fear of the unknown overwhelms them and they want to be back in the environment they are familiar with – even if it was abusive.

Change and transition can often be a trigger that takes traumatised children to a place of fear. For example, a new member of staff (teacher, youth worker, someone they've not met before) can be a huge change for them, as can a new activity or task, or a game they've never played before. Similarly, ending a task or activity that they have enjoyed can make them feel that if they stop now, they may never get to do this again! Why would they want to stop?

There is constant change in all our lives: starting new stages of education (nursery, pre-school, reception) each new year, and then, of course, the move to high school and college, new jobs, new houses. For vulnerable children, normal life-changes can feel like the end of the world.

Holidays and festivals throughout the year are a particular bugbear for me – and the lead up to Christmas, especially. So many changes in school activities, lots of excitement and hype everywhere you go, and, for our own children, difficult memories of their birth families, going into care, being separated from people. I personally love Christmas and the lead up to it because I can handle the excitement and the change, but, for my children, the whole of December is a time when we have to try to put in as much structure as possible to counterbalance the changes elsewhere.

Birthdays and anniversaries can also be a trigger point for children. One of our children especially struggles with birthdays. I'm not sure why exactly but managing his own emotions around this time has been a real challenge for him and us.

Trips and holidays can also be very stressful as the children struggle to regulate their very overwhelming emotions. I have suggested to schools, much to the surprise of some, that the children who struggle with change would find not going on a school trip much better than going. They don't need a trip to a theme park if that trip is going to cause uncontrollable stress for several days. The fear that the event generates for them and the difficulties for others trying to contain them outweighs the otherwise pleasurable experience of a theme park.

SO WHAT MIGHT YOU SEE IN CHILDREN WHO STRUGGLE WITH CHANGES AND TRANSITIONS?

You could probably write this list yourself if you are reading this with a particular child in mind and they have shown signs of struggling in this area at some point.

They may become upset, sometimes crying uncontrollably. It may also seem very disproportionate to the event at the time. They may also appear withdrawn and quiet about a particular event or activity, showing they are particularly anxious about it.

They may exhibit a deterioration or exacerbation in behaviour: they may be quite stressed normally but more so at a point of transition or they may be quite excitable under normal circumstances but even more so as a change takes place, a 'swinging from the chandeliers' kind of excited. This can also show up as an increased level of 'positive' behaviour – overly helpful or excessively friendly.

They may become more clingy and demanding than usual, showing extremely controlling behaviour, trying to make sure they will be safe and have their needs met. They may be consistently chattering to you about absolutely nothing at all – just wanting to know you are there and that you can see and hear them. They may also have a million questions about the experience if they are frightened about what might happen: 'Where are we going?', 'Who will be there?', 'What are we going to do?', and then repeating the same questions again and again.

Other areas of concern may become more prominent like eating issues, soiling and wetting, sleep problems and destructive behaviour.

Of course, children may not show any outward signs of distress around changes and transitions but that doesn't necessarily mean they are OK. Recalling the child with an avoidant attachment style, he does *not* want to be noticed so he will be working hard to avoid showing you any signs of anxiety.

WHAT ARE THE BEST WAYS TO HELP SUCH CHILDREN DEAL WITH THE CHANGES AND TRANSITIONS THEY FACE EVERY DAY?

Create a schedule or timetable for the child – in written or visual form – so that he can see what is coming up. You will need to be as clear as you can be about what may change: if you don't know whether or not something is happening at a particular time, then say that; it's better than the child expecting something to happen, only to find it doesn't.

Give the children plenty of notice that changes will happen. Children with a history of early trauma do not like surprises. Try to tell them as much as you can in advance, making sure that they are aware of the things that might not happen. For some children though the thought of something coming up can also send them into a state of panic so giving them as little notice as possible may be better. This is a tricky one and one you will have to gauge with the parents on what the best strategy is for that particular child.

When there are big transitions happening, such as moving years or groups within your setting, work out a plan with the parents or carers on how to involve the child in bringing about that transition. Make sure the parents or carers know all the variables around the transition so that they can work that into the way they communicate the transition to the child. You may want to get the parents involved in the transition like coming on the first day to help the child settle in.

A child may need additional visits to new places such as his new high school – visits where he will have the time and space to work through his fears with the appropriate personnel instead of trying to manage that in the presence of 30 other children.

Children may forget the details of a change or, indeed, block out the details if they are really fearful of the change. You will need to reinforce with written details – and photos if possible – to help them adjust to the change. Before my daughter started high school, I tried to take her to a few of the school's activities throughout the previous year to get her used to the school building. The school name cropped up in normal conversation, when something good was taking place at the school, for example, or when it was in the papers for something it or one of its pupils had achieved. Bringing the change into normal conversation ensured that it wasn't such a big shock for her later on.

Above all, remember that when a child reacts to a situation in a manner that seems to come out of the blue, it won't be out of the blue for him.

Something has led to his outburst, whether or not he is aware of what the trigger might be; something will have made him frightened, confused, frustrated or anxious about the change, the unknown and what might happen to him as a consequence.

Part 4

SOME FINAL THOUGHTS

Chapter 22

TRIGGERS

There are many triggers in our educational and recreational environments for children – things that may create a reaction in them, whether that is emotional, physical or mental. These triggers can send a seemingly content child into a rage at times. You may have seen this yourself: a child seems perfectly happy doing a task one minute, and then the next minute they have thrown their pencil down and refused to carry on.

This chapter is about those triggers: What are they? How can you recognise them? What impact do they have? What you can do to help children deal with these triggers?

I often hear people say something like, 'How can children remember what has happened to them when they were so young? They couldn't even speak or really know what was going on around them.' I, too, am amazed at how this seems to work.

Children who have been taken into care as babies, for example, still show signs of struggling as they grow up, even when it appears they did not suffer from prolonged abuse.

In some cases, these children seem to struggle more than those who went into care later in their childhood!

One of the books already mentioned is *The Primal Wound* by Nancy Verrier (2009). The author suggests that a baby's separation from its birth mother has devastating effects – it is indeed the primal wound that a child will then strive all of her life to recover from. She claims that the wound will always be there, but the way in which the child learns to adapt to that wound makes all the difference. Like being born with only one arm, the bearer has to adapt to lead a functioning life.

The idea that a baby cannot be affected by its circumstances unless she is old enough to understand does not hold weight. You may not be able to articulate or process what is going on for you at such an early age, but all your senses work. Smell, touch, sight and sound are available to you as a baby and this is what lingers. The memory of smells of a dirty, unhygienic environment can last, the sound of doors slamming and people being hit can last – and the over-riding sense of danger in a situation can last long after the danger has ceased.

Even when a child is too young to understand the depth of what is going on, there are memories that linger and last and which then become triggers in the future – which can take the child back to those feelings of being scared or hungry or cold.

If I mentioned certain familiar songs to you now as an adult, they might trigger distant memories for you – not all of them cognitive memories but feelings, sensations, emotions. We all experience these triggers so why is it so hard to believe that babies who have experienced a disturbed attachment cycle would react to triggers that take them back to a more uncertain and scary time for them?

One example of this is of the girl who cries whenever she smells a certain perfume on a teacher. That smell could be the perfume of her birth mother, caregiver, or the person she's not living with any more used. Another example is the child who cowers whenever she hears a male voice being raised but shows no reaction to a female shouting. Another is the child who shows an obsessive interest in a particular subject at school, like evacuation and rationing in World War II.

As you can see, triggers are a difficult area as they can come in any form: a sight, sound, smell, touch or a particular situation. It is also nearly impossible to know what will trigger a reaction in a child and how she might react. You could know that a child has not had much food, for example, and expect her to react to the history of rationing as mentioned above – but she may not! Or, to be more accurate, her reaction could be very well hidden.

Another area to consider is that there may be triggers in the tasks you ask children to do. The tasks may bring up feelings of inadequacy and low self-esteem. For example, a child may react aggressively to being asked to draw something – their reaction, whilst extreme, may actually be a response to not being able to draw or write. Those feelings of 'not being as good as other children' are, of course, common in many children but, for those who've experienced early trauma, those feelings may be magnified. They get frustrated easily and will opt out of tasks that appear too difficult for them. They may have been met with harsh reactions in the past (or the present) from parents who expected them to be able to do things much better than they actually can.

You have to remember when considering triggers for these children that uncertainty is always there for them. Living in an unpredictable environment leaves scars. The more they feel comfortable with people, situations and routines, the easier it is for them. Knowing what happens each day, where they need to go and who will be there are great comforters for them. Such children will often ask what is happening several times throughout every day, and will very often ask when the next meal is or what it will be – even while they are still eating another meal.

As mentioned previously, surprises are not such a great experience for children with a history of early trauma. They either can't cope with not knowing or the excitement becomes unbearable for them. For example, trips and swimming may become an obsession for them – always asking when it's happening, fixating on the details and logistics of a trip.

As with much of the content of this book, you could just as easily relate these aspects to children with secure attachments. It's worth mentioning, however, that what the anxiety is based on is very different for them, and how they process things is very different. A securely attached child knows they will get food at a certain time; they may ask when lunch is coming but, once they get the answer, they are content. For a child with an insecure attachment style, he may get the answer but it doesn't necessarily alleviate the anxiety and panic associated with not getting food. There are securely attached children who may react to loud noises such as balloons being burst, but they know it is a balloon and that it is nothing to fear – whereas a child who has experienced early trauma may associate something very different with loud, unpredictable noises and the fear does not subside as quickly or easily.

What kind of signs do you need to look out for? What might be common triggers for these children? As has already been said, triggers could be anything – and not what you would consider the most logical thing.

ONCE YOU KNOW WHAT TO LOOK FOR, WHAT CAN YOU DO TO HELP?

- Try to notice patterns of behaviours in the most vulnerable children: When does their behaviour change? What is happening at that moment or just before? Who was there or not there? What was expected of the child?

- Talk to the parents or caregivers about what might be possible triggers.

- Reassure the children that they are safe within your environment. If there are changes in routines, make sure the children know beforehand.

- As you are building trust with the children and helping them to understand what trust is, make sure you carry out the things you say you will do – they will notice inconsistencies.

- Communicate to the parents or caregivers any change in routines, such as tests or trips coming up.

- Think in advance about your programmes: what may be triggers for these children. Where possible, take the children's feelings into consideration. You may be able to change your projects slightly to accommodate certain children without adverse impact on others. For example, development and growth projects do not need to be around the child's history, such as bringing in baby photos. You could, instead, do the project around famous people or animals.

Chapter 23

PREVENTION IS BETTER THAN CURE

One of the objections I often hear against trying to bring in new strategies to help those who have experienced early trauma is the one around the time and resources needed to do the things suggested: to provide the one-to-one attention these children need, to create the time needed to understand them, to be able to treat some children differently to others – they all bring their own problems.

So why bother? Wouldn't it just be easier to treat the whole class or group the same – to be able to use the same rewards and sanctions for all?

In an ideal world, of course, that would work, but we all know that families are complex. The blended families that exist for these children are very much becoming the norm. Statistics tell us that 40 per cent of children will have experienced some kind of trauma before the age of 18 – with differing degrees of effect, of course. Remember that trauma comes from the external experience or threat of danger combined with the internal response. That's why you can be in a situation where two children experience the same event, one of whom copes well but the other struggles to come to terms with it.

The impact of trauma on children is the reason why we do need to bother. As we've said in earlier chapters, *their behaviour communicates need*, and when those needs are not recognised and not met in some way, a child's behaviours become much more difficult to manage.

Therefore, if we could look more at preventing the need for children to communicate in non-appropriate ways, it would be easier for the child, as well as for the rest of the class or group – and you as the adult.

The saying 'prevention is better than cure' can be re-phrased as 'it is better to try to keep a bad thing from happening than it is to fix the bad thing once it has happened'. How true. Of course, for traumatised children, bad things have already happened and may still be happening. But the additional negative things that could happen to them in school or in other settings outside the home – caused by the triggers that may bring back the early traumas – can often times be prevented.

This all sounds like common sense, but I know that, as an adoptive parent, understanding these things and then being able to pre-empt situations is very different and very difficult. As we've said before, the triggers may not be easy to see and the things you may think would not affect a child, do – and those you imagine would, may not.

My challenge to you, therefore, is to really spend the time to better understand children with a history of early trauma. If you can do that, you can empathise more and be able to really 'see' their needs.

When you can work to understand what your environment is like for such children, you can start to predict the anxiety they may feel when things change, when there are tests, when there are breaks, when relationships are involved, when there are expectations on them to fit in. To know that someone is thinking of you and has you in mind is a powerful thing for anyone, but especially for these children. Compare this to their past experience, when very few people, if any, had them in mind.

There are two books I'd like to mention again around this area. The first is *The Primal Wound* by Nancy Newton Verrier (2009) mentioned in the previous chapter. It is a controversial book in some ways and quite harrowing to read as it describes the depth of the emotional wound some of these children have experienced. The impact of that primal wound continues throughout their lives but the more understanding they have from adults, and the more connections they have with concerned adults, the easier it will be for them to start to heal. Very difficult stuff! But she makes many thought-provoking points about the effect of such early trauma on a child. This is important to know when you have children of this type in your settings, and when it's difficult to understand why they do some of the things they do.

The second book I'd like to remind you of to help you understand the possible behaviours of these children is an autobiography called *The Kid*, written by Kevin Lewis (2003). This is an incredible true story of a child brought up in terrible poverty, neglect and abuse. What is particularly amazing and significant about this, though, is the interaction he has with the schools he attends and with the teachers and other adults who try to help him. It is inspiring to see what a difference you can make in a child's life when the child is very confused about adults and the care he experiences from them. It is difficult to read – harrowing but very inspirational.

I would encourage you to read both of these books if you can, especially *The Kid*, as it is such an inspiring story of resilience and it connects us once more to why we want to make a difference in children's lives.

Chapter 24

COMMUNICATION IS KEY

Communicating with the essential people in the lives of vulnerable children is key. For those who are 'looked after', that will be their foster carers, social worker, maybe siblings they have contact with. For adopted children it will be their adoptive parents, grandparents and siblings. For those still in their birth families it is again the core families: mother, father, siblings, grandparents. Of course, as we know, there may also be step-parents, partners, and any number of combinations of adults involved in the children's lives.

There may also be other professionals involved: Child and Adolescent Mental Health Teams, psychologists, psychiatrists, occupational therapists, doctors, and so on. Many adults are involved in and have invested in their lives, which in itself must be very scary for children.

One of the areas around this that you will need to consider is the confidentiality issues for these children who have experienced early trauma and are the centre of attention for special care or provision. Of course, you will know your own codes of practice for data protection, but there are other aspects to consider. I am often asked about the background of my own children. Enquirers know they are adopted and want to know what happened to their 'real' parents? Were they abused? Do they see their birth families...? Whilst I understand the desire to want to know these details, we have to remember we are talking about real children's lives – their very intimate details that have already been aired in all kinds of public forums.

> *You only need to know a child is in care, or has been adopted, to realise that the child will have experienced some kind of early trauma.*

There are very few cases these days that are voluntary relinquishments and, even in such cases, the separation from the birth mother is traumatic in itself. You don't need to know any more details to know that all the things you've read so far in this book can help you to support such children as they make sense of their lives.

Adoptive parents can often feel that their adopted child 'belongs' to lots of other people. So many professionals are involved in making decisions for the child that, when he comes to live with his adoptive parents, it can take some time for the new parents to feel that they are the ones who know their new child the best. It takes a while to really feel that they are, in fact, the child's parents now and responsible for them.

This chapter is about communication between parents and providers. What does that mean exactly? We talk a lot about communicating with parents and working together with the child's best interest in mind, but sometimes this can be more difficult than it sounds. These children may not show the same behaviour at school and other settings as at home, and so the concerns we have may seem unreal to those working with them. Often my own children will work very hard all day to hold themselves together, and then once home the pressure releases and an angry, frustrated and sometimes uncontrollable child emerges.

Similarly, this frustration may be evident from the other point of view; as parents, we have many expectations of those working with our children. We can spend all the time in the world helping our particular child to adapt but we sometimes forget the great pressures on teachers and children's workers these days, with a class of 30 children to manage and teach – all with very different and complex needs. For those running clubs, this may be more in the hundreds!

So what's the answer? Again, no rocket science here, but we do need to communicate. This means honest, open communication where both sides are considered and where plans to work together for the good of our children are in place.

It is also very important to note that, when these children see 'their' adults working together, it instils in them some trust and faith in those adults.

They are so used to trying to segregate adults in their lives and may often say things to their school teacher like 'My mum doesn't give me any food' just so that they can get sympathy and some more food – when, of course, they have been given food but they've thrown it away or in fact eaten it already! It is very difficult for the teacher to know what is true and what isn't. The only way to find out more is to talk to the parents themselves.

There are also many seemingly insignificant things that happen at school or in clubs that parents need to know. An event may appear irrelevant to you as the person working with a child, but it may have a much deeper meaning for the child. For example, if you notice a child drinking excessive amounts of water, this can be connected to anxiety and fear communicated through distracting behaviours.

Also if parents notice a change in the child's behaviour at home, knowing that this is because there is a substitute teacher for a while, or that the classroom has changed in some way, can be very helpful for the parent in understanding the causes of the change in behaviour.

As we discussed in the previous chapter on prevention, knowing these things can make all the difference to parents as they work therapeutically with their child to help her make sense of events in her life. If there are tests coming up or there is a particularly sensitive subject being studied at school – such as identity and growing up – they need to be discussed thoroughly with the parents to help understand and contain the child's emotions during that time.

Working with birth parents is, of course, a different story. However, if you know there is trauma such as bereavement or loss through divorce, you can work to communicate with the parents involved. If a child has a relatively safe environment but experiences this kind of single trauma, she will usually have the foundations to be able to cope relatively well.

Noticing and understanding the symptoms you are learning about in relation to early trauma is a great step. When you recognise symptoms in a child you can try to work with the parents or carers – and also look to get others involved if necessary.

What follows are some ways to foster better communication with parents and carers of a vulnerable child.

At the beginning of each year, sit down with the parents or carers and discuss the child's needs – not just her academic progress, but also, more importantly, her emotional development. Review this throughout the year in regular meetings – this could just be 15 minutes at the end of each week. If you run a recreational club, do the same: meet with the parents to outline what kind of activities the child may be doing throughout the year and communicate on any issues either of you may see arising.

Look out for changes in a child's behaviour patterns – a change in anxiety levels, for example, and what it is related to: food, drink, friends, schoolwork, a specific activity? Make a note and discuss your observations with the parents or carers of the child.

Remember that what you see of this child may be very different to how she is elsewhere. It doesn't mean either scenario is not valid – both are a reflection of the child and how safe she feels in a particular environment. She may actually be feeling very anxious in your environment, but hiding it incredibly well. Talk to the child's parents or carers and believe them.

Be aware also that you are modelling trust as a safe adult in a child's life. It is very important that she sees you and her parents or carers working together to help her make sense of her world. It will be essential to her development as she learns to trust the adults around her.

Chapter 25

THE MOST IMPORTANT THING WE LEARN

For those in education or working with children in some way to help them develop, this chapter may be controversial.

My first question is: what is education? Why is it that all children are required to have an education? You might say that, for some, it would have been better if they had stayed at home. You may even admit, as I do, that the school years were *not* the best years of your life. What can you actually remember of the things you learnt at school? I'll bet much of what you remember was not out of textbooks, but out of experiences and relationships.

Whilst I believe and understand that learning is important, for those children who have so much chaos in their lives, learning – in the ways we teach at school – can be very difficult.

We must ask a second question though, not just 'what is education?' but 'what's the most important thing we learn?'

For traumatised children, there are many, many obstacles and barriers to learning anything at school or engaging in clubs and social groups.

We know that life is a cycle: if our parents have good, strong parenting from their parents, they pass that onto us and then we parent our children the best we can, to enable them to grow, function in life and parent their own children adequately. However, when you see children who have not had a good experience of parenting, nine times out of ten, their parents have also experienced poor parenting – they are these little children grown up.

Therefore, if you can break the cycle for such children then there is great potential for them to grow up in a different and more positive way: to be able to function in life, make good decisions, hold down jobs and relationships, contribute to the world and in time create their own families that grow up to do the same.

So what is the most important thing to learn? If you broke down the curriculum taught in schools today and picked out those things that help children to be emotionally resilient, resourceful and secure, how much would there really be? Could you honestly say that much of what we learn at school helps us to do that – to be resilient, resourceful and secure?

I came across a school recently that I want to bring to your attention: Rockingham Primary School in Corby, England. They run their school in quite a different way. Their focus is on the whole wellbeing of the child. They are in a deprived area with 45 per cent of the 250 children with some kind of special educational need, 23 per cent of which fall into the behavioural, emotional and social needs categories.

When I heard of this school, the head at the time Juliet Hart said:

> There is a common language that is shared across the whole staff team and we recruit people that share that philosophy. The basic Theraplay principles of nurture, engagement, structure and challenge underpins every class. In our Ofsted inspection report, our duty of care was recognised as outstanding. (2010)

One of the class teachers, Donna Johnson, tells how the days look – that they are well structured and revolve around activities that involve taking turns, getting on with each other, adapting according to the children's needs, relieving anxieties and teaching the children that it is all right to make mistakes.

As has been covered in previous chapters, if children feel a high level of anxiety it is almost impossible for them to learn and to be able to be creative and independent in their play. Having a holistic approach to a child's wellbeing means that the state they are in when approaching a task is even more important than the outcome of that task.

In other words, teaching children calming techniques, how to manage their emotions and being self-aware is just as important as the mechanics of reading and writing.

As you grow up into an adult, the skills needed to remain positive against adversity, to build a strong character and to make good decisions are paramount.

Not to say of course that you are not already bringing these great practices into your educational environments, but it is important to recognise just how essential it is for children who have experienced early trauma to know that academic achievement is not the most important achievement. Having a strong sense of security in yourself, knowing that you can make a difference in whatever you do with your life, is an amazing thing to realise.

There are constraints, of course, within our educational system. We've talked over these pages about these children who have experienced early trauma and how they need a different kind of care and support. For example, being able to keep children in lower classes until they are ready to move up is very beneficial for children who are usually acting at an emotional age different to their chronological age. Being able to go back and build those blocks of development again would be a great part of their healing process.

Of course, for those of you not in education but working with children in some other capacity, you may have all the flexibility to bring in new ways of working and reaching these children – brilliant! Take the opportunity to do that. Many of the techniques and principles in this book are beneficial for all children, not just those with attachment difficulties.

There are also tendencies to avoid singling children out as different by keeping them back a year, for example, or treating them differently due to their trauma. However, we have to realise that they *are* different – they will already feel different to their peers. Think about those early experiences in the first few years of life as the foundations in a wall – the bottom bricks of which the whole building rests on. Traumatised children have bricks missing or damaged: they may not have had consistent food, sleep may have been disturbed, love may not have been shown, stimulation and play may not have been present. Once you then start to pile bricks on top to help them, the foundation is not solid and they find it incredibly hard to accept.

We need to go back and help children relive and experience those essential elements of development. Some things are impossible to replace, of course, but finding the things you can and helping the children concerned to do that would be another key to engaging with them.

What, then, can we take from this chapter? Emotional development and learning to 'cope' with life is essential for a child's development. Children who do not have this support at home, or who didn't in the early formative years, will struggle to function effectively or to break the cycle of emotional trauma from generation to generation.

In order to do this you may want to look at strategies within your setting that could help. Research other schools or groups such as Rockingham Primary School; there are many where they look at the needs of the whole child and aim to bring in specific services where needed.

There are many therapies and techniques that can help children learn and connect. Some you will know about; *Theraplay* is one as mentioned in this chapter. *Peer massage* is another tool that helps children with self-regulation and being able to connect with others. Music and movement therapies help children who have experienced trauma to become more aware of their body, feelings and emotions. Drumming is also proving to be a great experience for children.

Consider the overall settings approach to emotional and social wellbeing. Academic aspirations, along with the constraints of target-setting, can make it difficult to focus on the other aspects of learning, but consider the possibility that you may be one of the few contacts a child has with a positive adult. What can he learn from you and from your approach to him? How would his future be different if he could learn resilience, resourcefulness and a strong sense of self and wellbeing?

Chapter 26

WHAT'S SO WRONG WITH REWARDS AT SCHOOL?

Something I'm asked time and again, whilst doing training for schools, is how can we use rewards effectively with children who have experienced trauma? Well, there are a few fundamental questions we have to ask ourselves when thinking about rewards:

- What are we rewarding children for?

- Why do we feel the need to reward?

- What are we hoping we will achieve when we reward them?

The whole concept of rewarding good behaviour is rife in our homes and schools but where did it come from? Is it a throwback to the harsher days of never praising children for when they did something well, of only reprimanding them when they stepped out of line? When you look this topic up on the internet it's littered with articles and techniques around how to reward positive behaviour in children and ignore the bad.

However, what about when children have had a difficult start in life, they don't have the strong foundation that nurtured children have had, and they don't have the secure base of a safe parenting structure to come back to when they go off and explore? Their worlds, in short, are upside down to other children's worlds. So why do we then insist on treating them the same? They do not understand why you are rewarding them for something and it gives them mixed and damaging messages sometimes.

For example, our first question: *what are we rewarding children for?*

In a classroom we talk about good or appropriate behaviour. We want a child to sit in a certain way, do the tasks asked of them quietly, be polite with people, not hit other children, etc. All things that we feel are acceptable and appropriate in our society – the niceties of how we interact with each other. So what about a child who struggles in these areas? They can't sit still due to the hyper-vigilance they feel about whether they are safe or not, they have little impulse control, their cause-and-effect thinking is not developed and they have no empathy. To expect them to follow the rules, when they haven't been taught them and many times don't have the tools they need to be able to comply, is unrealistic.

Rewarding children (or punishing them by not rewarding them) for things they cannot do sometimes sends the message that they must be so bad that they can't control their emotions and actions. To see other children getting their stickers and sweets for something they feel is impossible for them to do only compounds that feeling of inadequacy and worthlessness.

In previous chapters we've talked about how children who have experienced trauma feel at the core of their being that *they are bad* – not that they do bad things but that they are bad. The toxic shame associated to this feeling is too much for them to bear sometimes. When we then reward them for something we think they have done well, two things happen in them. First, they do not believe you so they will prove you wrong by doing something they know you will disapprove of, like hitting another child. Second, they think that you are lying to them, as they totally and whole-heartedly believe they are bad, it's engrained in them, and this can start to erode the trust you are building with them.

The way our educational system is set up these days is around behaviour modification techniques – getting children to behave in the way we as society deem is fit. What happens in the midst of this is there are masses of children who don't fit the mould – in fact I would go so far as to say no child fits a mould. They are all unique, different, individual and as such should be treated so.

I can hear the cries of 'easy for you to say, you don't have to teach a class of 30 children all with different complex needs,' and of course that's true but that's my point – the system is set up in such a way to meet our needs as adults and teachers, not to meet children's needs. I've heard recently of many schools that are moving to open-plan classrooms. I don't see how this can help children's concentration and attention. For children who have experienced trauma especially the noise and chaos will not help them to learn but in fact it will hinder them greatly.

What should we be rewarding children for then, if at all? Well, I believe we need a different approach. Instead of trying to modify children's behaviour and push them into a mould of what we think is appropriate, maybe we should be encouraging them to explore their emotions and feelings more. Instead of being afraid of anger and aggression, find ways to help the child integrate that into their whole person. I've always been a volatile personality and have struggled for years with my temper, so much so that at times it makes me feel that *I am bad* – in who I am. I wish that I'd have been taught at school how to face my feelings and deal with my anger in such a way that it was not swept under the carpet or seen as a nasty trait, but as part of the whole human experience.

Imagine what a child would feel like if they were praised for being able to express their feelings, or encouraged to wrestle with their failure and disappointments – how different would they be as adults, I wonder?

So on to our second question: *why do we feel the need to reward children?*

We are told that what you focus on is what you get and I can see that. The more you comment on the negative things and complain about how awful something is, the harder it is to get yourself out of that place. However, for children who have experienced trauma especially we must always put their needs before ours. I think as adults we feel that if we don't praise every single thing we're not supporting and encouraging children. I'm not saying of course that we should pick on their difficult areas and make them feel rubbish. What I am saying is that we need to look at why we struggle so much with this whole area of rewards. Whenever I've spoken about this on training, invariably someone struggles with this concept of giving low-key praise and not linking it to the action. We feel that the point of rewarding is so that they do that behaviour again – behaviour modification – but the key element to remember with these types of children is that their behaviour is communicating a need. They are not naughty children; they are scared and anxious children showing that in ways that we find difficult and that are unacceptable in our societies.

What I will say about praising children is that we need to make sure we are building up their self-esteem. This will take a long time and baby steps – when you go in all guns blazing and tell them how fantastic their singing is and they should be on *The X Factor* you have no idea how that information will be received. They need small doses of praise and affection that builds their resilience and gives them a sense of who they are and who they can be.

This brings me to my final question: *what do we hope to achieve by rewarding them?*

In the traditional sense with our reward charts and sliding scales of behaviour charts we are hoping they will toe the line and conform to the 'right' ways of behaving according to us. However, you have to remember they have probably experienced a very different environment to other children and what they know as normal and acceptable is not what you or other children will think. For them it may be acceptable to hit someone when they can't get their own way, or to demand food from other people. Don't forget as well that they are very self-reliant and will do whatever it takes to get their needs met. That's not behaving inappropriately if what they feel they need is that food that someone else has or they will die. We cannot understand the depth of emotion they may feel around something that terrifies them.

Most primary schools use a variation of a sliding scale, where the children all start out in the green square at the start of the day then move to amber if they don't keep the rules, then to red. This doesn't send a great message to vulnerable children. If a child is frightened and incredibly upset about something, so much so that they can't sit still or do their times tables, our response should be compassion and support, not to move them down the scale. Also of course for children who need attention being in the red is what will give them the attention – they don't care if it's good or bad attention.

I said earlier that these children are upside-down children – the 'normal' rewards and consequences don't work with them so there needs to be a new approach. The main way we can reach these children is through relationships. Relationships are where things have gone wrong for them in the past and relationships are what can build their self-esteem and change the way they see themselves and the world around them.

It's a process of moving from one belief – such as we must reward specific behaviour for a child to learn that's how to behave – to a radical concept that if we could build a strong relationship with the child, encourage expression and integration (knowing that we *all* struggle with the full range of human emotion) and find ways to help a child feel safe and feel good about themselves and their worlds, then I believe we would have really helped a child to grow to be a well-rounded, resilient, functioning member of society.

Chapter 27

INNER AND OUTER RESOURCES

When thinking about the keys to helping children who have experienced early trauma I can't help but put in something about the resources you will need to call on. Progress can often be slow – and you feel that what you are trying to do with a child is hopeless and that he may never change.

> *There are two types of resources you will need – those within yourself and those outside of yourself.*

There is a theory called *The Slight Edge* written about by author Jeff Olson (2013). The general premise is that we always look for the big leaps of change, the instant result and the thing that will turn something around radically. However, what is often needed are the baby steps that will eventually unlock something for us or for the children we work with.

When you think about the children in your care you may have the desire for them to change or develop by a rate of 100 per cent within a year. When you say it like that it seems impossible – to change by such a quantum leap. However, can someone change 0.003 per cent each day? That's three-tenths of a percentage each day. If you did that every day then by the end of the year you would have improved by over 100 per cent!

The tiny steps of progress you see each day are massive in terms of the long-term impact for these children. Every day is a chance to move closer to that improvement target, be it their emotional, intellectual or social development.

One of the inner resources you will need is tenacity – the determination not to give up on the troubled children you work with. However small the progress may seem, at times, they will be inching their way forward, with your help.

Another inner resource needed is trust in your own intuition – your gut instinct. It's that compulsion you experience about something – it may be a concern that a child is at risk, or that he needs a different approach to others, or that you need to go against what's expected for the sake of the child.

Many things can stop you acting on your gut instinct, such as your own personality and your tendency towards action or inaction. Some of us, for example, procrastinate; we know what we must do but are afraid to do it or we try to put it off. Words from an inspirational quote by Marianne Williamson inspires me:

It's our light, not our darkness, that most frightens us. (1992)

What if we did step out and really go for something big – what could be possible?

For those of you who have a tendency to 'over-think', I'd recommend a book called *Blink* by Malcolm Gladwell. He looks at the instant reactions we have to situations, which we then talk ourselves out of through 'over-thinking'. Here's an extract from the book to get you thinking more about not thinking so much:

One of the stories…is about the Emergency Room doctors at Cook County Hospital in Chicago. That's the big public hospital in Chicago. A few years ago, they changed the way they diagnosed heart attacks. They instructed their doctors to gather less information on their patients: they encouraged them to zero in on just a few critical pieces of information about patients suffering from chest pain – like blood pressure and the ECG – whilst ignoring everything else, like the patient's age, weight and medical history. And what happened? Cook County is now one of the best places in the United States at diagnosing chest pain. (Gladwell 2005)

From what you know right now of the children you work with, what would be the few critical things you would zero in on? What is important in their lives right now? Is it friendships, security, learning to read or being able to express themselves? How can you become laser-sharp focused on securing that progress for them?

What about the outer resources? One of the main areas is around a theory called Kaizen. When used in the business sense and applied to the workplace, Kaizen refers to activities that continually improve all functions, and involves all employees from the top of the business to the bottom. In our educational settings, Kaizen is about continuous improvement, looking at areas that need changing and being open to new ideas and approaches to how you work and teach.

My challenge and request is that, as those involved in education and working with children, you continuously strive for more knowledge and understanding of these children who have experienced early trauma – their progress and how what they lack in their lives has affected their development in so many areas. Kaizen is a daily process, not a once-a-year review. There is so much to notice and learn each day.

Throughout this book there have been many references to resources – books, websites, theories and so on. I would really encourage you to pursue knowledge in this area, whether you have contact with many children in the 40 per cent category of those who have experienced trauma, or you just want to make sure you are ready and well informed for when you do. As a starting point, I have listed a number of books and websites in the bibliography section of this book. Have a browse… and the final word goes to Alvin Toffler, author of *Future Shock* (1999):

> Learning is an approach, both to knowledge and to life, that emphasizes human initiative. It encompasses the acquisition and practice of new methodologies, new skills, new attitudes, and new values necessary to live in a world of change. Learning is a process of preparing to deal with new situations.

Chapter 28

A WORD OF WARNING

I want to give a word of warning when working with children who have experienced trauma. The work you put into these relationships and the investment you make into supporting and helping them can be quite draining. Due to the complexities of their needs you can find yourself impacted greatly by them, and this can become overwhelming for you as the person closest to them.

As parents we talk about secondary trauma – a term used to describe the stress resulting from helping or trying to help a traumatised or suffering person. Prolonged interaction with a child who has experienced severe neglect and/or abuse can take its toll on you as an adult. If you are getting close enough to the child to really make a difference to them, you will definitely be affected by their lives, their story and the impact it has had on them in their current lives.

The other condition that can develop is known as 'blocked care'. This is a relatively new term used by Dr Dan Hughes, which describes the impact of prolonged involvement with children who cannot respond to your endeavours to connect with them emotionally. Usually in relationships we rely heavily on the response of the other person to make us feel good about the relationship. However, with children who are struggling to respond emotionally, it can be a very exhausting and frustrating experience, which can leave you unable to give the care you want to.

In a recent article on brain-based parenting, Dan Hughes and his colleague Jonathan Baylin commented:

> In short, we knew what these hurt kids needed from their caregivers: the ability to stay engaged and open with them, especially when the kids were 'going defensive' and resisting the closeness they deeply needed but instinctively avoided. (Baylin and Hughes 2012)

The reason I'm mentioning this as a closer to this book is that these feelings and experiences, whether secondary trauma or blocked care, are not only common to adopters/foster carers but they are also prevalent in those who are working on a long-term basis to meet children's needs. Once you can recognise this and take action to look after yourself you will be able to return to helping the child deal with their anxieties and make sense of their lives.

Some of the things you might recognise as symptoms of secondary trauma:

- feelings of anxiety and even dread before spending time with them

- being exhausted physically and/or emotionally after spending prolonged time with them, which can result in illness

- becoming irritable at every little thing they do

- feeling a sense of powerlessness in their company

- being aware of them controlling every aspect of your contact with them

- intrusive thoughts and/or second-guessing

- sadness and/or anger

- poor concentration

- fearfulness and/or shame

- absenteeism and/or detachment

- normal stress symptoms – headaches, sleep difficulties, change in appetite, tense muscles.

It can be a very difficult thing to admit to yourself and your colleagues as you can feel alone and guilty about your feelings towards the children or feel inadequate and not able to cope within your role.

> Traumatic stress can make staff ashamed about their strong reactions and uncomfortable about burdening colleagues or loved ones with their pain. (Chris Siegfried, of the National Child Traumatic Stress Network 2008)

The symptoms of blocked care are slightly different. Dr Dan Hughes talks about parents who want to do the best for their children, and want to parent them therapeutically using PACE as we discussed in Chapter 8, but for some reason are not able to (Hughes and Golding 2012). I understand this feeling perfectly. I know much of the theory behind parenting traumatised children but in the heat of the moment, and given the fact that it is a relentless task, finding the energy and desire sometimes to meet their needs can be tough. At times it can feel like you don't want to meet their needs – that the care you want to give them is blocked (by you or by them).

WHAT CAN YOU DO TO COMBAT SECONDARY TRAUMA OR BLOCKED CARE?

- Acknowledge that it is there – if you feel any of the symptoms above you may be suffering from this.

- You may need to take yourself away from the child for a while. This can be difficult if you have formed a strong bond with the child and they have started to trust you. However, you need to be able to look after yourself in order to then be able to focus on the child's needs again.

- Get some help with processing your feelings and how the child's trauma makes you feel. Talking to other people in similar circumstances can help. Also you may need more professional help from therapists or people who can guide you in dealing with your feelings.

Sometimes the feeling of blocked care can be with the most 'compliant' child, not the child who is extreme in their behaviours. Very often the avoidant child keeps you at arm's length and will not respond to your care. They can be very self-reliant, as they have needed to be, which means they may listen to you but then do something completely opposite. This can be wearing and the feeling that they are deliberately ignoring you or manipulating you can be difficult.

Like the great philosopher Smurfette said when discussing Passive Aggressive Smurf – 'Passive Aggressive Smurf is nice when you're with him but you feel bad when he leaves' (*The Smurfs* 2011) – the same can be said of these children. You can't put your finger on it, they may not have done something to make you feel upset with them, but something feels off about your interaction with them.

Above all remember that these children's strategies to survive can be very well engrained within them. They are not consciously aware of their impact on you and the need to survive is greater than their desire to make you feel better.

This is why working on understanding your own attachment style is paramount to working with these children. Anything you may struggle with in your own life will be magnified by your involvement with these sensitive time-bombs who are triggered to explode at any given moment.

So my final words to you are this – look after yourself, be kind to yourself and those around you, continue to try to connect with these children and see their pain. They need you so much, as well as all the other adults in their lives. Without us they will only follow the same cycle they have come from. They need all of us working together to help them break that cycle and become functioning, well-rounded adults.

Thank you for your dedication to these children – know that it is the most valuable work you do and you are making a huge difference!

ABOUT THE AUTHOR: NICOLA MARSHALL AND BRAVEHEART EDUCATION

BraveHeart Education was established by the author Nicola Marshall in 2011 to help and support those working with vulnerable children – whether they are looked after, adopted or in challenging home environments.

BraveHeart Education came about through many interactions with adoptive parents and foster carers whose children struggle within our educational settings. As a result of these conversations Nicola started travelling around the country training schools and those working with children on how to understand children who have experienced trauma. This work is so important and needed.

What qualifies her to talk about this subject, you might ask?

Nicola's career background is in management and personal development. Trained and certified as a coach she has spent the last five years helping others in all walks of life to achieve their goals, through training and coaching. In May 2008 her life changed dramatically when she adopted a sibling group of three with her husband. That threw her into the world of attachment and trauma with a bang. Living with the realities of children who have experienced trauma has been a roller coaster. Nicola has studied theories and strategies to help them, attended many courses, read numerous books and generally immersed herself in this world.

Nicola fundamentally believes that without people really understanding what the world is like for vulnerable children they will not be able to become resilient enough to break the cycle in their lives. That is her main aim for her children and the purpose of her work – to enable children to become functioning, well-rounded adults who can contribute to society and be equipped to parent their own children in the best way possible.

If you would like to get in touch there are a few ways you can connect. The BraveHeart Education website is regularly updated with training schedules and blogs (www.BraveHearteducation.co.uk) or you can contact Nicola by email any time at nicola@bravehearteducation.co.uk

BIBLIOGRAPHY

BOOKS

Barrett, M. and Trevitt, J. (1991) *Attachment Behaviour and the School Child: An Introduction to Educational Therapy.* Oxford: Routledge.

Bomber, L. M. (2007) *Inside I'm Hurting: Practical Strategies for Supporting Children with Attachment Difficulties in Schools.* London: Worth Publishing.

Cairns, K. (2002) *Attachment Trauma and Resilience: Therapeutic Caring for Children.* London: British Association for Adoption and Fostering.

Cooley, C. H. (1902) *Human nauture and social order.* New York: Scribner's.

Gladwell, M. (2005) *Blink: The Power of Thinking without Thinking.* New York: Little Brown and Company.

Griffiths, J., Pilgrim, T. (2007) *Picnic in the Park.* London: British Association for Adoption and Fostering.

Hart, J. (2010) 'Regulation, Regulation, Regulation,' *Adoption Today.* Available at www.fosteringfamiliestoday.com, accessed 24 June 2014.

Hughes, D. A. and Golding, K. S. (2012) *Creating Loving Attachments.* London: Jessica Kingsley Publishers.

Lewis, K. (2003) *The Kid.* London: Penguin.

Matthew, J. (2012) *After Adoption Conference,* Seminar. Cardiff, 24 April 2012.

Middleton-Moz, J. (1990) *Shame and Guilt: The Masters of Disguise.* Florida: Health Communications, Inc.

Mooney, C. G. (2010) *Theories of Attachment: An Introduction to Bowlby, Ainsworth, Gerber, Brazelton, Kennel & Klaus.* St Paul, MN: Redleaf Press.

Olson, J. (2005) *The Slight Edge: Secret to a Successful Life.* Smyrna TN: Momentum Media.

Perry, B. and Szalavitz, M. (2006) *The Boy Who Was Raised as a Dog and Other Stories from a Child Psychiatrist's Notebook—What Traumatized Children Can Teach Us About Loss, Love, and Healing.* New York: Basic Books.

Perry, B. and Szalavitz, M. (2010) *Born For Love: Why Empathy is Essential—and Endangered.* New York: Harper Collier Books.

Post, B. (2009) *The Great Behaviour Breakdown.* Palmyra, VA: Post Institutes & Associates.

Stern, D. (1985) *The Interpersonal World of the Infant.* New York: Basic Books.

Toffler, A. (1999) *Future Shock.* St Louis, MA: Turtle Back Books.

Verrier, N. (2009) *The Primal Wound: Understanding the Adopted Child.* London: British Association of Adoption and Fostering.

Wallen, D. J. (2007) *Attachment in Psychotherapy*. New York: Guildford Press.

Williamson, M. (1992) *A Return to Love*. New York: Harper Collins.

Winnicott, D. W. (1971) *Playing and Reality*. London: Tavistock Publications.

WEBSITES

Baylin, J. and Hughes, D. (2012) 'What Neuroscience is Teaching us About Connecting With Our Kids.' Psychotherapy Networker. Available at www.psychotherapynetworker.org/magazine/currentissue/item/1647-brain-based-parenting, accessed on 2 June 2014.

California Department of Education [CDE] (2005) 'Foundation: Cause-and-Effect.' California Infant/Toddler Learning and Development Foundations. Available at www.cde.ca.gov/search/searchresults.asp?cx=001779225245372747843:g pfwm5rhxiw&output=xml_no_dtd&filter=1&num=20&start=0&q=self%20 regulation, accessed on 2 June 2014.

FASD Trust (2014) *The Pregnant Pause*. The FASD Trust. Available at www.fasdtrust.co.uk/cp9.php, accessed on 2 June 2014.

Forsyth, J. (2012) *Statement: Definitions of poverty should not distract from growing and urgent crisis affecting poorest children in the UK*. Save the Children. Available at www.savethechildren.org.uk/2012-06/statement-definitions-poverty-should-not-distract-growing-and-urgent-crisis-affecting, accessed 2 June 2014

Online Dictionary by Farlex. Available at http://medical-dictionary.thefreedictionary.com, accessed 16 June 2014.

Harlow's Study on Dependency of Monkeys, video clip, YouTube. Available at www.youtube.com/watch?v=OrNBEhzjg8I&noredirect=1, accessed 2 June 2014.

Maslow, A. H. (1943) *A Theory of Human Needs*. Classics in History of Psychology. Available at http://psychclassics.yorku.ca/Maslow/motivation.htm, accessed 2 June 2014.

NSPCC (2014) *Statistics on Child Neglect*. NSPCC. Available at www.nspcc.org.uk/Inform/resourcesforprofessionals/neglect/statistics_wda89685.html, accessed 2 June 2014.

Poole, C., Miller, S. A. and Booth Church, E. 'Ages and Stages: Empathy, how to nurture this important gateway to a social and emotional growth.' Available at www.scholastic.com/teachers/article/ages-stages-empathy, accessed 16 June 2014.

Sonkin, D. (2009) *Attachment Theory and the Brain: An interview with Dr. Daniel Sonkin*. Neuronarrative Available at http://neuronarrative.wordpress.com/2009/01/12/attachment-theory-and-the-brain-an-interview-with-dr-daniel-sonkin/, accessed 2 June 2014.

Siegfried, C. B. (2008) *Child Welfare Work and Secondary Traumatic Stress*. The National Child Traumatic Stress Network. Available at www.nctsnet.org/nctsn_assets/pdfs/CWT3_SHO_STS.pdf, accessed 2 June 2014.

WEBSITES

RESOURCES
UK

www.bravehearteducation.co.uk

Nicola Marshall's website – UK site to help support those working with vulnerable children in education. Training events and resources available through this site.

www.bemyparent.org.uk/features/what-is fasd,295,AR.html

This site is a UK site part of BAAF with information about adoption and fostering. The specific link relates to information on Fetal Alcohol Spectrum Disorder.

www.fasdtrust.co.uk

This is the website of the Foetal Alcohol Spectrum Disorder Trust based in the UK. The site provides lots of information and resources on FASD.

USA

www.youtube.com/watch?v=apzXGEbZht0

This is a link to a video on You Tube showing the Still Face Experiment done by Edward Tronick an American Professor of Psychology.

www.postinstitute.com

This is the website of Bryan Post an American Child Behaviour Expert. It is full of resources – books, articles, videos about Attachment and managing difficult behaviour in children.

www.scholastic.com/teachers/article/ages-stages-empathy

American website with resources for teachers on child development.

www.attach.org

Website from the Association of Treatment and Training in the Attachment of Children. American site with lots of different resources available.

http://reactiveattachmentdisorderlife.blogspot.co.uk

A blog site written by a Children's Therapist in the States on Reactive Attachment Disorder.

www.childtrauma.org

> Dr Bruce Perry's Website – an American Child Psychiatrist specializing in Brain Development.

Canada

www.attachmentcan.ca

> Website for the Attachment Association of Canada giving details of professionals, conferences, information and resources.

Australia

www.attachmentparentingaustralia.com

> Australian Parenting Attachment website giving details of resources and information on Attachment.

INDEX

DATE